ZOONOTIC

A NEW PARADIGM FOR DESIGNING
SUCCESFUL VIRAL BUSINESS STRATEGIES
CAROLE LAMARQUE

Lannoo
Campus

This book was originally published as *Zoonotic, de formule voor een extreem succesvolle virale businessstrategie*, LannooCampus, 2021.

D/2021/45/80 – ISBN 978 94 014 7514 3 – NUR 801

Cover design: Ben Meulemans
Interior design: Gert Degrande | De Witlofcompagnie
Translation: Ian Connerty

LannooCampus Publishers is a subsidiary of Lannoo Publishers,
the book and multimedia division of Lannoo Publishers nv.

LannooCampus Publishers
Vaartkom 41 box 01.02   P.O. Box 23202
3000 Leuven   1100 DS Amsterdam
Belgium   Netherlands
www.lannoocampus.com

CONTENTS

PART 2: HOW DO YOU BECOME A ZOONOTIC? 81

PART 3: HOW CAN YOU FIGHT A ZOONOTIC? 178

FEATURES

Throughout this book there will be a number of recurrent feature sections.

EXPERT OPINION

In this feature, I test my ideas on people I respect and who, in my opinion, can provide you, as a reader, with important added value, because they all have expertise in the relevant domain.

UNDER THE MICROSCOPE

In this feature I take a closer look at a number of sensational viral business strategies with Zoonotic characteristics, using seven questions as a test to explain their success. These are also useful indicators for your own viral business strategy.

INSIGHT

In this feature, I take a brief detour to provide you with some supplementary background information that will give you deeper insight into certain aspects covered in the main body of the text.

ONE MORE THING

Steve Jobs and my favourite TV detective Columbo both used this seemingly banal phrase as a prelude to announcing something important. I make grateful use of the same phrase to introduce examples of companies or applications that have become successful as a result of the corona pandemic.

Introduction

WHAT DO I WANT TO ACHIEVE WITH THIS BOOK?

In 2020, we all made our acquaintance with 'The Big One' – or was this just the dry run or a sign of something worse to follow? Be that as it may, we all experienced at first hand how powerfully a virus can strike and how quickly the resultant pandemic can spread around our planet. Above all, we learnt how disruptive the consequences can be. Even Dr Peter Piot, a world authority in the field of viral epidemics like AIDS and ebola, said in a podcast (for *De Tijd* newspaper) that he was completely surprised by the speed and the massive societal impact of the crisis, quite apart from the dramatic medical aspects of the situation.

My starting point for this book is my contention that by studying and learning to understand this and other pandemics, it is possible to discover valuable lessons for your own viral business strategy. I am firmly convinced that companies that conquer the world with viral innovations are not just 'lucky'. On the contrary, and exactly like a pandemic, there is a predictable pattern to their success. Economic principles are not a matter of coincidence. Successful companies follow a clear strategy and have a specific mindset. To attribute something to 'chance' means, in my opinion, that we have simply not yet discovered the correlation between the various underlying factors. Usually, that only happens after the event. Even so, that does not mean that it is a pointless exercise. A knowledge of these underlying patterns can often still be of use later on.

In the following pages I will describe the approach taken by companies that conquer the world with their viral business strategies and innovations. I call this strategy 'Zoonotic'. Of all the world's many viruses, the Zoonotics are amongst the most powerful. A Zoonotic is a new and previously unknown virus that occurs when two known viruses combine in a host (which serves as a Superspreader) to create something completely new.

For example, let's imagine that a 'bird' and a 'bat' both infect a host – a 'pig' – with their own individual virus. The pig immediately becomes a Superspreader for their combined viruses. The Cheetah makes a Zoonotic out of this new combination in the form of a new product or a new service, with which to start its exponentially increasing conquest of the world.

> There are clear parallels between the way a
> biological virus works and a viral business strategy.

A Zoonotic infection is known as a zoonosis. The Spanish flu, which conquered the world by making grateful use of soldiers and refugees returning home after the end of the First World War, is a famous example. However, a business Zoonotic does not make use of trains, boats and planes, but exploits the potential of the world wide web to spread itself. In recent decades, it was primarily the SARS-CoV-2 virus that alerted us to the potential danger of zoonoses. 'The outbreak of this virus [COVID-19] should not really come as a surprise,' wrote Barbara Debusschere in *De Morgen* newspaper. 'Nature is full of little beasties, germs and pathogens. According to an estimate by the Global Virome Project, there are something like 1.67 million undiscovered viruses currently circulating in mammals and birds, half of which can be dangerous for humans. When the Chinese virologist Shi Zhengli, who has been analysing coronaviruses in bats for the past 16 years, discovered that two people in Wuhan were infected with a virus that was similar to the SARS virus, she immediately warned her team that this could become a major problem. Because these experts know all too well that infectious zoonoses are now spreading faster and faster.'

With this kind of infection there is usually an intermediary host, most typically a bird or a mammal. A thousand or so years ago, the measles virus was transferred to humans via cattle. The plague virus (commonly known in medieval times as the Black Death) used rats as its host. The HIV virus was passed on to humans by chimpanzees.

'But Carole,' I can hear you say, 'isn't it a bit macabre to seek inspiration in a virus that has cost hundreds of thousands of lives world wide and caused incalculable damage to both the economy and to society at large?'

I can understand that some of you perhaps have doubts about my approach. So let me be clear: my inspiration has nothing to do with the deadly effect of the virus, but with the extremely efficient and disruptive impact of a Zoonotic. I am not arguing in favour of a strategy that sows death and destruction! Quite the reverse, in fact. While a biological Zoonotic always has fatal consequences, a business Zoonotic has two possible outcomes, depending on your intentions and your guiding principles. This is what Jonathan Berte of Robovision refers to as 'Good Karma versus Bad Karma'. In instances where things are clearly moving in the wrong direction – in other words, when Bad Karma gains the upper hand – I use the term Predator Zoonotic. Of course, one of the things you need to remember about Karma is that, at the end of the day, it always gives you your just deserts!

> Is it not the dream of every company to find an unstoppable
> – but people-friendly – viral business strategy?

I want to challenge you to use the intelligent spreading strategy of a Zoonotic as inspiration for an extremely successful, sustainable and viral business strategy for your company. As a business leader and marketeer, I feel a strong compulsion to draw as many positive lessons as possible from the current worldwide pandemic. That is simply my nature as a hyperkinetic, positive-thinking entrepreneur!

There is also another reason why I am extra-interested in viruses: I have twice been a victim of their insidious power. On the first occasion, this was almost fatal. For weeks, my life hung by a slender thread. This was followed by months of uncertainty, a feeling that has never completely left me. More recently, in 2019, I was infected again during a study trip to... China, of all places! So perhaps it is hardly surprising that I am fascinated by the intelligent strategies used by these micro-

EXPERT OPINION

Professor Dr Marc Buelens

Emeritus professor, Vlerick Business School

The limits of a metaphor

My clients know that I like to challenge them. For my part, I also like to be challenged – and certainly by someone like Professor Dr Marc Buelens, emeritus professor of the Vlerick Business School, who is renowned in his field for his sharp and critical mind, with which he analyses and dissects management and organisational theories with scientific precision. This is his reaction to my idea about using the Zoonotic as a metaphor for a viral business strategy.

'If, without wishing to compromise my intellectual integrity too far, I look dispassionately at the message of someone who has invested her soul in a fascinating new marketing concept, I am forced to conclude that many others before her have also found inspiration in the most diverse images, models and studies. Markets have been compared with doughnuts, the 4 Ps, frogs, the 7 Ss, networks, and water running through a pipe system, to name but a few. If grown adults are convinced that they can find inspiration for their business ventures in such matters, who am I to gainsay them? Carole has a remarkably wide experience of her field. Consequently, there is a strong likelihood that she has developed a form of intelligent intuition, which allows her to see what others cannot (yet) see. However, formulating intuition and channelling it into models is always a difficult task and the question then becomes whether or not any criticism applies to the basic insight or to its subsequent formulation.

A model – let's call it a theory – only becomes relevant if it makes it possible for us to predict in advance whether players in the market will be successful (or not) because of their adherence (or not) to that theory.

A metaphor does not need to be perfect. All it must do is identify and illustrate the key elements. Viral marketing and the reference to a unique phenomenon in medical science – zoonotic pathogens – allows us to illustrate something that it was not possible to illustrate as tellingly before; namely, lightning-fast technology, social media and many other facets of the "winner takes all" marketplace. It illustrates the success of some (I emphasise the word "some") hybrid technologies, of some bizarre and unique successes, etc., etc.

A strong metaphor also needs to make clear when its precepts will not be applicable, and these areas must be more than mere trivialities. So let me briefly make misuse of the virus world to show how such an approach can be misleading. Let us look at things from the point of view of the virus. To begin with, there are an awful lot of them. One website tells me 100,939,140. Another says that they are more numerous than the stars (although this I doubt). But let us say that, as an entrepreneur, I am a virus, one of the 100 million. So why am I not COVID-19? In that case, the story becomes less fun. Most viruses are anything but successful. On the contrary, they lead quiet and largely hidden lives. So why take an exception as the basis for a model? You can push this kind of reasoning a stage further. It is also easy to defend yourself against a virus: just wash your hands and keep a safe distance! In this way, your product will never reach me, because I, like most consumers, will do the customer equivalent of applying basic hygiene and social distancing rules. So what can persuade me (and them) not to do this? That is a fascinating question, and one that I would like to discuss in more detail with every group of managers and entrepreneurs. So the virus metaphor is a strong one. But no more than that.'

scopically small intruders. This book is my way to turn my personal misfortune with viruses into a positive and meaningful experience.

I want to show you how insight into the power and the spreading speed of a Zoonotic can inspire you to develop your own extremely successful viral business strategy or, if that is not possible, how you can defend yourself – by 'flattening the curve' – against a Zoonotic attack in your market. In contrast to a biological virus, the objective of a commercial Zoonotic strategy is to have positive effects for both your company and your customers. Primarily, it is your competitors who need to be most concerned about your Zoonotic approach and will suffer most from its consequences.

> In my book *Unfair Advantage* I introduced the metaphor
> of the Cheetah. With this book I want to build on that image by
> challenging the Cheetah to move beyond the confines of its
> familiar savannah landscape and expand its territory much more
> quickly than ever before.

To complement the worthwhile considerations of Professor Dr Marc Buelens, I would like to emphasise that in the first instance my purpose with the Zoonotic metaphor is to offer you a conceptual model that will stimulate and inspire you by helping you to structure the unknown. This is easiest to do by using a striking and instantly memorable metaphor that strikes a chord not only with major international companies, but also with the many tens of thousands of small and independent entrepreneurs, managers and NGOs.

> I want to encourage people to act positively for change,
> rather than passively watching and waiting for failure.

In the first part of the book, I will describe precisely what I mean by a Zoonotic, not simply by outlining a basic model, but above all by illustrating my arguments with a series of diverse examples, ranging from Uber via Duolingo to Botox! In this way, you will discover that a Zoonotic always begins with a new and previously unknown combination of elements, which, from the moment they combine, will expand at an exponential speed, just like a prowling Cheetah, until the world has been conquered.

In the second part, I will describe how you can become a Zoonotic. Using your core – which I call your Unfair Advantage – as a starting point, I will show how you can give the kick-off as a fully fledged Zoonotic leader, supported by a super-flexible Zoonotic team. To complete this section, I will challenge you to make use of the seven exercises that will allow you to get moving in the right direction.

Finally, in part three, I will outline how you can best defend yourself against a Zoonotic attack. Initially, you will need to navigate like a Cheetah in a sandstorm, where your quick and flexible reactions will hopefully enable you to avoid the threat or at least allow you to limit the damage.

EXPERT OPINION

Kate Raworth

University of Oxford
University of Cambridge

The doughnut as a metaphor

The doughnut model, as described by Kate Raworth in her book *Doughnut Economics*, is a superb example of a powerful, visually simple and coherent metaphor. The hole in the middle of the doughnut symbolises the people whose basic needs in terms of food, health care, education, etc. are not met. The innermost ring of the doughnut indicates the lowest social and societal boundary, while the outermost ring delineates the ecological limits of our planet. The central core of the doughnut is the zone where social and economic needs are fulfilled for as many people as possible. This is 'the safe and just space for humanity', as Raworth calls it. The challenge is to move the people who are currently in the 'hole' (= shortfall) into the doughnut zone, but without exceeding the ecological capacity of the planet (= overshoot). The fact that Raworth indicates twelve lower social limits and nine upper ecological limits means that this doughnut model can also be used as a policy instrument.

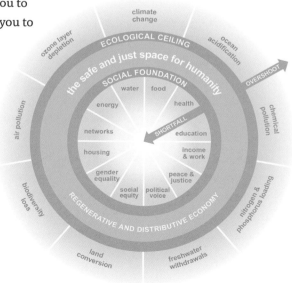

Source: *Doughnut Economics*, Kate Raworth

PART 1

WHAT IS A ZOONOTIC?

This is a book about successful viral business strategies that have a biological virus as their role model. In this first part, you will discover what a Zoonotic is – with different examples to make the concept more concrete – and will explore the five basic characteristics of a Zoonotic virus with me, namely:

1. A Zoonotic combines two existing viral successes to create something totally new.
2. A Zoonotic makes clever use of influencers.
3. A Zoonotic often begins its existence as a dormant, almost invisible entity.
4. Once it starts to expand, a Zoonotic grows at an exponential speed.
5. A Zoonotic regards the entire world as its territory.

"

The battle against COVID-19 is like a new world war, but this time we are all on the same side.

"

Bill Gates

1

A NEW AND PREVIOUSLY UNKNOWN COMBINATION

Precisely because it makes use of a new and previously unknown combination, a Zoonotic can initially remain under the radar and escape attention from others. The new combination does not relate in any way to existing systems, knowledge or insights. With a biological Zoonotic, this results in an often fatal weakening of the inadequate immune system of human beings. With a business Zoonotic, it results in an extremely disruptive policy model, which often has fatal consequences for the competition.

If innovation is described as the process by which something of value is created through the application of a new solution to an existing problem of significance, then I would regard a Zoonotic as a hyper-innovator.

The diagram below is a model-based depiction of the Zoonotic metaphor. The bird is the carrier of Unfair Advantage 1; the bat is the carrier of Unfair Advantage 2. Together, these Unfair Advantages form a new combination in the pig, which acts as the Superspreader. The Cheetah is the new Zoonotic offer: the new product or service that will conquer the world.

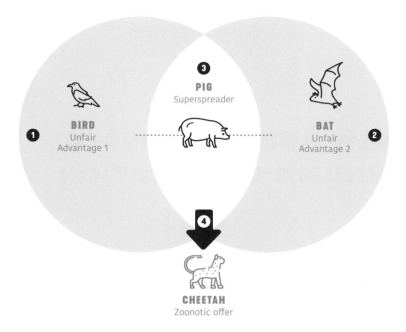

BIRD
Unfair
Advantage 1

PIG
Superspreader

BAT
Unfair
Advantage 2

CHEETAH
Zoonotic offer

A new and previously unknown biological virus can succeed in remaining under the radar and subsequently infect the entire world, because such viruses have the most remarkable survival mechanisms. They make intelligent use of hosts to reproduce and spread themselves. However, if it wants to secure its own future, it is important for a virus not to be too efficient or aggressive. For example, the Ebola virus is so deadly that it risks jeopardising its own survival, because ultimately it becomes hard to find live hosts to ensure its continued spread. In the business world, Uber is a good example of an over-aggressive business Zoonotic, which resulted in some countries and cities banning the company. Personally, I am not a great fan of this kind of business culture.

An over-aggressive Zoonotic can destroy its own market.

Sometimes, a business Zoonotic needs to take a 'chill pill' to temper its aggression, so that it can come back stronger than ever when the time is right. Take, for example, Google Earth. Their approach is not 'in-your-face' aggressive, but has still been sufficiently Zoonotic to rapidly conquer a market. According to Google's own figures, they now cover 98 percent of the inhabited world. Conclusion? If you want to become a successful Zoonotic, sometimes it is a good idea to rein in your ambition so that you do not bring about your own downfall by being too eager.

ONE MORE THING

LINGUISTIC ZOONOSIS

The corona crisis certainly stimulated our creativity. One of the results was a plethora of new word combinations, from lockdown parties via cough-shame to balcony solidarity. But there is one combination that has become more popular than all the rest and has spread around the world in different languages like a true Zoonotic. In English, this is the combination of 'cuddle' and 'buddy', to describe the people with whom you can have close contact. In Dutch, this translates as 'knuffelcontact', which was chosen as 'word of the year' in Flanders, in part because of its warm connotations. It was first coined by the Belgian Minister of Health, Frank Vandenbroucke, on national television, thereby creating the basis for this linguistic Zoonotic.

What are successful Zoonotics like?

Before I take you step by step on a voyage of discovery through the Zoonotic success formula, it may be useful to start by giving a number of concrete examples. In this way, it will become clear what I mean when I talk about a Zoonotic and how this viral business strategy is capable of turning an established market completely on its head.

> UBER

Uber caused a veritable pandemic in the taxi market. The business model of the classic taxi companies came under extreme pressure. The great advantage of Uber is its ease of use: you register just once, press a button and your taxi is ordered! The initial anger and resistance of the taxi sector has since resulted in the development of creative apps that now allow customers to access classic taxi services in a more user-friendly way. For example, the Traveller Connect application not only makes it simple to book and pay for a taxi, but also makes it possible to follow its actual position. In my opinion, Uber's Achilles' heel is their seeming lack of respect for their self-employed drivers. To be honest, this callous attitude makes me really angry.

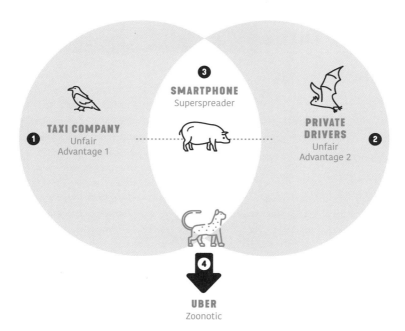

TAXI COMPANY
Unfair
Advantage 1

SMARTPHONE
Superspreader

PRIVATE DRIVERS
Unfair
Advantage 2

UBER
Zoonotic

EXPERT OPINION

Scott Galloway

New York University

Uber is 'capital light'

According to Scott Galloway, one of the major trump cards of Uber is the way the company uses the assets of others as a lever. The drivers are not on the payroll and Uber does not need to invest in a car fleet, so that it also saves on insurance and maintenance costs. Much the same is true of Airbnb, which does not invest in buildings, personnel, catering, cleaning, etc. As a result, these companies are less capital intensive, so that they are able to downscale more quickly in the event of a crisis such as the corona pandemic, simply because they have fewer fixed costs. Airbnb is the strongest brand in the travel and hospitality business, with more than 7 million rooms in its portfolio. That is more than all its competitors combined. Did you know that in percentage terms they employ more technical experts and engineers than Amazon, Lyft or Uber? As a result, their business model is totally different from those of traditional hotels.

As already mentioned, there is a danger that Uber has become an over-aggressive Zoonotic, so that some cities and even whole countries have banned the company, as can be seen on the following map of the world.

Where Uber operates, and where it's been shut down

● Cities where Uber operates ● Cities or countries where Uber is banned or is being challenged

Portland, Ore.
Dec. 8
Sues Uber, says it
violates city laws

Nevada
Nov. 26
Statewide ban

**Los Angeles,
San Francisco**
Dec. 9
Prosecutors sue
over consumer
protection issues

Colombia
Nov. 22
Car-booking apps
that don't belong to
registered taxi firms
are prohibited

Toronto
Nov. 19
Asks court to shut
down Uber, citing
safety concerns

Brussels
Apr. 15
Says UberPop
is illegal

Paris
Aug. 4
Court says
Uber can't
charge by
the kilometer

Netherlands
Dec. 8
Halts UberPop
service

Berlin, Hamburg
Sept. 26
Says Uber drivers
lack required license

Spain
Dec. 9
Country-
wide ban

Thailand
Nov. 28
Regulator says
car-booking apps
face fines

New Delhi
Dec. 7
Bans Uber after a driver
is accused of raping a
passenger

Rio de Janeiro
Dec. 8
Says Uber is illegal and
threatens to take drivers' cars

Sources: Uber, Bloomberg reporting
GRAPHIC: ALEX TRIBOU / BLOOMBERG GRAPHICS

> WAZE

The Waze algorithm is a Zoonotic in the mobility and transport market. Since the advent of TomTom and Garmin in 2004, every vehicle user has become familiar with the advantages of a GPS system. Satellite navigation is now taken for granted. In addition, radio stations broadcast up-to-date information about traffic jams, speed traps, etc.

Waze is a Zoonotic that combines both of these existing advantages – GPS and actualised information – and makes use of the omnipresent smartphone as a Superspreader. Whereas people used to be satisfied with the combination of two separate systems (GPS + radio), they have now discovered that it is much more convenient to have access to the combined information via a compact device that everybody always has in their pocket or handbag. Thanks to Waze, I am now able (like all its many other users) to navigate easily and safely through unknown cities and landscapes. I can still remember vividly the way things used to be: me, with my brand-new driving licence in my purse and my clammy hands gripping the steering wheel, driving through Brussels for the first time with a copy of the

De Rouck street plan guide open on my lap! I had one eye on the map and one eye on the chaotic traffic. It was miracle that I never hit anything – and was still able to find my way to my destination!

Thanks to Waze, it is now almost possible to navigate with your eyes closed – please, don't take that literally! – and you also know how long your trip will take, how you can avoid the traffic jams and what other obstacles you may encounter along your route.

It is this ease of use that has quickly turned Waze into a worldwide success. That and the fact that every user helps to ensure that the information becomes more complete and more up-to-date, so that the service continues to get better and better. The system's creators no doubt think it is fantastic that all of us are helping their product to become more and more efficient!

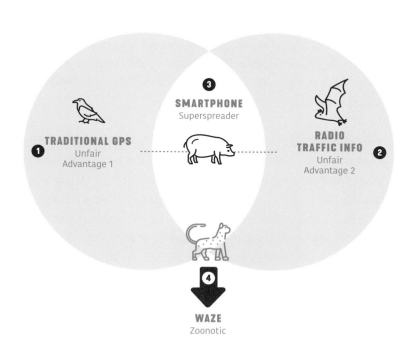

> BOTOX

Botox is a Zoonotic in the anti-ageing market. Anti-wrinkle creams have been known since the times of the ancient Egyptians. The first commercial anti-ageing lotion was launched in 1889. In the meantime, this market for lotions and creams has grown into a worldwide business, estimated to be worth 53 billiondollars in 2019. In recent decades, plastic surgery has also entered the battle against ageing, making possible both limited and drastic aesthetic correction to your body. This market is expected to have a worldwide turnover of 22 billion dollars by the end of 2023.

Botox came onto the market in 2002 as an innovative and simple cosmetic treatment, where by a chemical product was injected with a common-or-garden syringe, providing improved results that were much faster than lotions and creams and much less painful (and expensive) than plastic surgery. Because the effects of Botox are immediately visible, every Botox user instantly becomes a Superspreader for the treatment (assuming, of course, you are a fan of super-smooth and super-tight facial skin). What's more, I am not simply talking about vain women of the Kim Kardashian variety, but also about equally vain men like Putin and Berlusconi. Speaking personally, I cherish my wrinkles as a visible part of my life story and who I am.

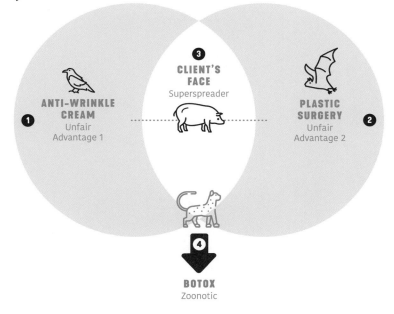

> CO-WORKING

Co-working is a Zoonotic in the office premises market. What is an office? A place where people work primarily with their heads, rather than their hands. This kind of work location has existed for hundreds of years and is generally known and accepted worldwide.

At the same time, there is a growing number of people nowadays who are working from home or who at least want to reduce the time they waste travelling to and from the office. This has coincided with the emergence of the concept of the sharing economy, in which digital technology is making it increasingly possible for people to lend, share or buy things from each other. The internet also makes it possible for people to come into closer contact with each other than ever before, no matter where they are in the world.

This combination of working from home and working at the office led to the development of co-working and co-working locations: places where both individuals and groups can work together without the need to pay full rent for the hiring of the necessary space. In this way, the sharing economy became the Superspreader that allowed co-working locations to go viral.

> SMARTWATCH

The smartwatch is a very evident Zoonotic in the wearables and technology market. Although smartphones (including Blackberry and the Psion palmtop computer, combined with a Sony Ericsson telephone) have been available since the end of the 1990s, it was not until the arrival of the iPhone in 2007 that the major breakthrough occurred. In the meantime, the iPhone has become the undisputed king of the Superspreaders. Since it made its appearance, it has not only totally transformed the world of mobile telephony, but also mobile communication and access to the internet in general. Nowadays, we have the net, email, SMSes, photos, videos, music, television and so much more quite literally at our fingertips.

It is truly amazing how in such a short space of time the smartphone has silently and with consummate ease worked its way into the everyday lives of billions of people worldwide. The device has now become an extension of ourselves. I must confess that I belong to the growing group of smartphone adepts who can no longer imagine life without it. Do you know that feeling of unease, when you have left home and suddenly realise that you have forgotten your smartphone? You do? Well, I get that feeling as well. A typical symptom of addiction? Very probably – and you can take the word 'addiction' literally: research has shown that every 'ping' or vibration of your smartphone releases dopamine – the 'feel-good' hormone – in your brain.

Of course, the wristwatch has been around for much longer, not only as a way to tell the time, but also as a fashion accessory that technology has made ever more perfect through the years.

The bright idea of combining smartphone technology with the elegant simplicity of the wristwatch led to the creation of a new Superspreader – and so the smartwatch was born. It not only lets you know how late (or how early) it is, but also gives you information about your health, your level of physical effort, how well and for how long you are sleeping, and the hundred and one other things that you can find on a smartphone. You can even personalise the watch face and change it as often as you like, so that it can look like you are wearing a new watch each day.

The success of the smartwatch should not be underestimated: in 2019 the sales of Apple Watches far outstripped the sales of the world-famous Swiss watches by 30.7 million to 21.1 million, according to Strategy Analytics.

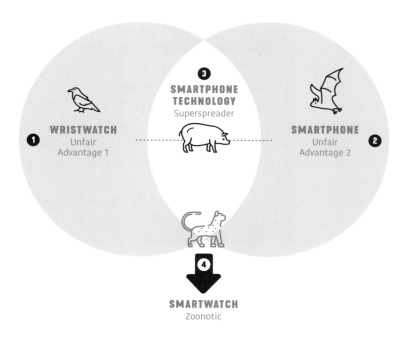

> TESLA

In the automobile market the electric car is unquestionably a Zoonotic. Elon Musk is not the inventor of electric-powered vehicles. In fact, the first application of this kind dates back to the 19th century! However, it is above all the massive improvement in battery technology combined with the development of a network of recharging points that has created a new Superspreader. It is this evolution that Tesla has been able to exploit. The fact that Tesla is much more an advanced technology company than a traditional car manufacturer, and therefore has a completely different way of thinking and working, is the key factor in explaining why Tesla is maintaining its lead in this market. Have you got an Elon Musk in your company? Or are you your own Elon Musk? Are you going to be the new Superspreader who ensures that your product, service or brand creates a disruptive pandemic in your sector?

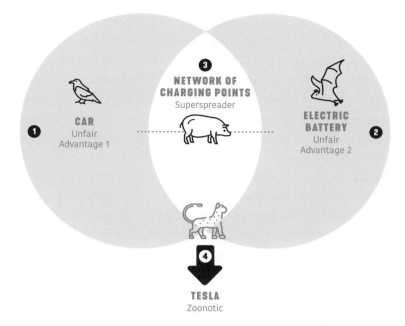

③ NETWORK OF CHARGING POINTS
Superspreader

① CAR
Unfair
Advantage 1

② ELECTRIC BATTERY
Unfair
Advantage 2

④ TESLA
Zoonotic

> BEYOND MEAT

Beyond Meat is a budding Zoonotic in the booming market for vegetarian food. The world meat industry is estimated to have a likely value of 1.5 trillion dollars in 2022. Since the 1950s, which were marked by a post-war period of economic growth and prosperity, meat has become a fixed element in most people's daily diet. However, during the past decade more and more questions have been asked about the possible negative impact of this industry, not only on the environment but also in terms of animal cruelty, hygiene and safety, as highlighted in the increasingly frequent outbreaks of epidemics such as swine fever and mad cow disease.

As a result, many people are now going in search of meat substitutes. Although these products based on vegetable proteins have improved in quality in recent years, the majority still do not regard them as a flavoursome and viable alternative for real meat. For my part, I have been a confirmed vegetarian since 1983, but even I realise that as long as there is no vegetable-based option that looks like meat and tastes like meat, the carnivores among us will remain unconvinced.

Or that, at least, was the case until now. Because waiting in the wings there is a nascent Zoonotic that in the years ahead will most likely represent a serious threat to the meat industry. Working together with University of Missouri professors Harold Huff and Fu-hung Hsieh, CEO Ethan Brown succeeded in 2011 in producing 'chicken meat' that actually contains no chicken. Instead, it makes use of a combination of soya beans, carrots and a special production technique. Admittedly, the success of this initial experiment was limited, but the inventors refused to give up and their further efforts resulted in a non-meat hamburger that has exactly the same texture and flavour as the 'dripping-with-blood' versions that you can get at your local neighbourhood McDonald's (the 'blood' in this case being provided by the use of red beetroot juice). Since then, they have also developed a meatless sausage that has been equally well received by a growing number of traditional meat lovers. This has all the makings of a Zoonotic that can rapidly accelerate the spread of meat substitutes, which will have a positive effect on world health, climate change, the availability of natural resources and animal welfare.

But perhaps this new Zoonotic will not come from the US after all, but from China, where in recent years the annual consumption of pork has risen from 68 million tons to 95 million tons. Under the pressure of climate challenges, the COVID-19 pandemic and the increasing incidence of African swine fever, the price for the pork that the Chinese so love to eat has risen by 30 percent. As a result, more and more families are now prepared to consider less costly alternatives. This offers a huge opportunity for David Yueng and his Green Monday company, which is working on the development of a pork substitute under the name OmniPork. It will be interesting to see in the years ahead who will be the winner in this particular race. One thing is certain: if I was working in the meat industry, I would take these emerging Zoonotics very seriously indeed – and make sure that I had a suitable response to the threat they pose.

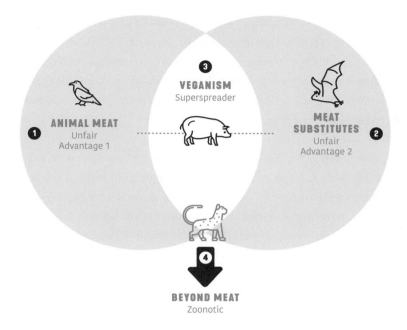

> DUOLINGO

Duolingo is a language course with Zoonotic qualities. More than 300 million people have already downloaded the application on their smartphone. Its biggest plus point is the way it continually encourages you in a playful manner to keep on practising your chosen language. To do this, Duolingo makes use of a short but stimulating format that is also typical of platforms like Instagram or Facebook. A fun emoji reminds you that it is time for your next exercise. The app has been a big hit with people of all kinds: from Bill Gates and Khloé Kardashian to Syrian refugees in Turkey. Turkish was the fastest growing language in 2020 on the Duolingo app in the United States, while Spanish is still the most popular language worldwide.

People have always had access (and still do) to personal language teachers, but this method is time-consuming, expensive and has a limited range of possibilities. Likewise, self-study methods such as Assimil and online language courses are nothing new. The strength of Duolingo is its simplicity (it only requires a few minutes of practice each day) and its playful style, which is in keeping with typi-cal social media usages. You can also adjust the speed of learning to reflect your personal preferences, although in general the results are quick, which acts as an extra motivation. With its compact and energising communication techniques, it encourages you to keep on making progress in short and simple steps. It also gives you the feeling that you are spending time on your smartphone that is not wasted, but actually results in something useful.

Perhaps after reading this you will get the urge to brush up on your knowledge of Spanish? Or even to learn a completely new language? I wouldn't be surprised, because Duolingo is an out-and-out Zoonotic. Its growth is staggering. Duolingo has more than 40 million monthly active customers and offers a range of 39 dif-ferent languages. The company has discovered that in Hawaii many of the resi-dents are keen to learn the traditional Hawaiian language. Similarly, Navajo has also enjoyed a boost in popularity.

It is worth noting that 40.5 percent of Duolingo's customers belong to Generation Z (born between 1997 and 2012). Their most popular language? Japanese!

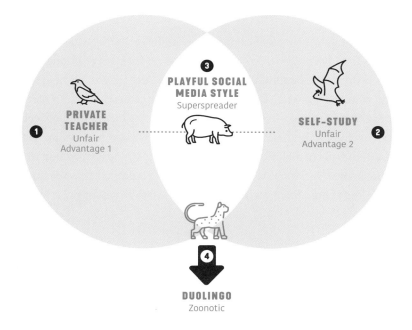

> ZOOM

Skype is undoubtedly the Zoonotic that initially made free online video calls so popular. Started in 2003, the app enjoyed exponential growth in 2005. As a result, 'skyping' became an expression frequently used and understood in everyday language. Skype still has 74 million active users, but in recent years it has allowed its digital thunder to be stolen by competitors like Zoom (2011) and Microsoft Teams. The strength of Zoom resides in the simplicity with which it can be installed and used. It offers numerous useful aids and tools that can help to facilitate online consultation, such as screen sharing that allows multiple people to view the same document or PowerPoint, or the sharing of sound from your computer, so that everyone can listen to and see the same video clip. Additionally, it is also possible to divide up the various conversation partners into smaller groups for separate consultation, whilst at the same time still being able to chat continuously with all the participants. A simply symbol system further allows you to give and receive feedback or to change moderators quickly and easily. Skype seems to have lost the battle against Zoom, in part because of the bugs it still contains and the advertising messages that irritate many of its potential users.

Similarly, Microsoft Teams now offers a better alternative than Skype for Business. Microsoft Teams is more than a means of communication; it is a powerful and effective instrument for working together efficiently within Teams. Microsoft Teams positions itself as an 'apphub', since with the help of Microsoft 365 (previously Microsoft Office) it makes it possible to combine various applications, such as Sharepoint, OneNote, Planner and dozens of other Microsoft apps, at a single location.

A smartphone with a built-in, high-quality camera generates a further rapid spreading of both systems, since it releases you from being tied to your computer. In addition, COVID-19 has ensured that the use of video calls, video conferencing and webinars has increased at an accelerated pace among a wider public.

So how did a niche platform like Zoom manage to beat larger Zoonotic competitors like Apple, FaceTime, Google Meet, Cisco Webex and Skype?

1. Zoom is free (at least for the first 40 minutes).
2. Zoom is much easier to use: you do not need to download an app or set up an account and the platform can be used in various different ways.
3. Zoom is cloud-based, so that upscaling is easier.
4. Zoom's virtual background protects privacy, because your interior is not visible.
5. Positive stories and memes from Zoom users ensured fast recognition.
6. The brand name is catchy, informal and comfortable to use ('Shall we Zoom?').
7. Skype stagnated because its mother company Microsoft gave priority to Teams.
8. Schools and professional users were the first to embrace Zoom.
9. The fact that influencers like Charli XCX and Lady Gaga appeared in *Saturday Night Live* Zoom video parties provided valuable extra publicity.

As is so often the case in Silicon Valley, its user-friendliness and the speed with which it was launched turned out to be the Achilles' heel of Zoom, since this meant that insufficient attention was paid to the matter of security. This problem has now been rectified, but it remains an open question whether Zoom can continue to win the battle against online giants like Microsoft or Facebook/ WhatsApp. It might even be the case that by the time this book is in your hands the decision has already been made.

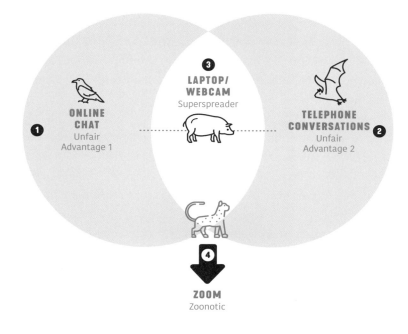

These ten examples illustrate perfectly the seemingly simple but oh so powerful 'hop, skip and a jump' principle of a Zoonotic. Later, I will make you aware of the more specific essential characteristics of a Zoonotic, so that you can learn how to think and act like one. In this way, I want to bring out the Zoonotic leader in you.

ONE MORE THING

THE LITERARY HERITAGE OF THE PLAGUE

We know from our own experience in recent times that a pandemic can also have surprisingly positive side effects. That was also the case in 1593, when many of the leading rivals of William Shakespeare died during the plague epidemic that hit London during that year. The huge subsequent demand for new plays gave the young Shakespeare his breakthrough – following which he changed the world of theatre and drama forever.

How predictable is a pandemic?

We can already be certain that the human race will be threatened by new pandemics in the future and that our high degree of mobility over long distances means that it will be very hard to localise these outbreaks. However, it is impossible to predict precisely when and where the next pandemic will occur. All the statisticians can do is attempt to predict how a pandemic will evolve, once it has manifested itself. During the corona crisis we have seen that there are two different ways of approaching this matter.

On the one hand, there are economic models that focus on disruptive innovation, such as the one developed by Bart Van Looy and Kristof Decock, two business economists attached to the Catholic University of Leuven's Flanders Business School. This model first began life as part of a doctoral thesis analysing the sale of electric cars. On the basis of sales figures for the period 2011 to 2017, Van Looy and Decock developed a model for predicting the level of sales in 2018. Their predictions turned out to be 98 to 99 percent accurate. When the coronavirus burst onto the scene, they decided to apply their model to statistics relating to the pandemic. 'There was an urgent need for an accurate model, even though there were many unknown factors,' says Van Looy. They first examined the three parameters that are applicable to every S-curve. If you assume that these can all move in any direction, you end up with something like half a million possible curves. On the basis of the first actual figures, they then chose only the curves that corresponded by 98 percent with the real progression of the epidemic.

On the other hand, there are also models developed by epidemiologists, such as Professor Dr Anne-Mieke Vandamme, attached to the Laboratory for Clinical and Epidemiological Virology (Rega Institute), also at the Catholic University of Leuven. These models approach the progress of the pandemic with a great-er degree of caution, precisely because there are so many unknown factors involved. The epidemiologists know from experience that a pandemic does not al-ways evolve in accordance with an simple S-curve. As a result, they are only prepared to make predictions when they have sufficient actual data at their dispos-al. This is in contrast to economists, who have fewer qualms about the high degree of uncertainty in their models. One of the things that the economic models were able to predict accurately was the likely date of peak infection rates –providing you do not count the wave of infections in residential care homes – but not the likely height of that peak. At that point, the epidemiologists were not yet ready to make such bold statements. If, however, you include the infections in the care homes, the economists' predictions were not correct, neither about the date nor about the height of the peak. As soon as two epidemics overlap, the increase in infection no longer follows a standard S-curve. This is something that epidemiologists can take into account, but not economists.

EXPERT OPINION

Prof. Dr Anne-Mieke Vandamme

Laboratory for Clinical and Epidemiological Virology (Rega Institute), Catholic University of Leuven

Models are not only of use in pandemics

'These models can also be useful for measuring other trends and possibly for making predictions, if it seems that the trends in question are evolving expo-nentially, as is the case, for example, with some aspects of climate change or per-haps even of growing populism. In these instances it is also important for policy makers to take account of a possible ex-ponential evolution, so that they can take action before it is too late. The problem is that most people have no idea what an exponential growth process involves. As a result, a quasi-invisible trend can sud-denly explode, at which point it is already too late to take the necessary remedial measures.'

Even so, economic models continue to have value as a tool that allows policy makers to take certain decisions and to demonstrate afterwards, if the projected trajectory fails to materialise, that their decisions did effectively help to slow down the evolution of infection.

ONE MORE THING

MIRROR, MIRROR ON THE WALL...

People's desire to play sport and/or work out when the fitness centres were in lockdown provided some interesting new opportunities for creative innovators. For example, YouTube work-out films became super-popular and the number of fitness apps spread like wildfire. Of course, having a piece of physical work-out apparatus in your house is much more motivating than any YouTube film or app. The best of these devices was unquestionably Mirror, which was launched by the New York start-up of the same name. At first glance, Mirror is just... a mirror. Is there any better motivation than seeing just how unfit you have become? Perhaps. Perhaps not. However, the really smart thing about this particular mirror is that it contains a LED screen that puts you in direct contact with a personal trainer. And when your training session is over, all you need to do is just roll up your mat and admire the beneficial effects of all that exercise in your mirror!

(Source: *De Tijd*)

2

A ZOONOTIC IS LIKE A CHEETAH ON THE PROWL

A Zoonotic successfully manages to lead a camouflaged existence, so that the virus initially remains under the radar. This dormant period can last for a number of months or even years.

It begins with a singularity

According to the 'Big Bang' theory, our cosmos began with a singularity. That is the name that scientists give to the absolute starting point from which everything – matter, time and space – first originated. In more general terms, a singularity is something unusual or out of the ordinary; something for which the normal rules and laws are no longer valid or can no longer be applied. It is the period of calm before the storm, when all the processes of what is to follow are in preparation but for the time being remain unseen. Occasionally, you might see a rippling on the surface of the sea as the tip of a shark's fin briefly cuts through the water, before disappearing just as quickly as it emerged, only to break through again with full force at the right moment, when it is ready to attack in what Accenture refers to as a Big Bang disruption.

For me, singularity is a metaphor for the long journey that your future Zoonotic Cheetah needs to make through the dry and empty savannah. If you read the stories of people like Jeff Bezos, Steve Jobs or Elon Musk, you will discover that they were also isolated and alone at the start of their journey. There were huge risks, plenty of blood, sweat and tears, and numerous ups and downs – not to mention piles of cash – before they were finally able to force the ultimate breakthrough. The singularity is the process in which, in all quietness and unnoticed by others, you create, adjust, amend and improve what you hope will become your Zoonotic. It is the period in which you go in search of the 'partners in crime' who can help you to further develop your idea, as well as seeking out those who can give you the necessary financial resources to make your dream come true. It is the incubation phase in which the new idea, still kept hidden and seldom mentioned, gradually takes shape. It is only later, when everything is ready, that you bring it out into the open and hope to experience an exponential acceleration phase: the famous hockey-stick curve.

SHARK FIN MODEL

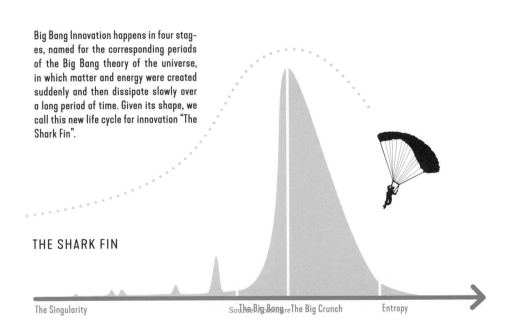

Big Bang Innovation happens in four stages, named for the corresponding periods of the Big Bang theory of the universe, in which matter and energy were created suddenly and then dissipate slowly over a long period of time. Given its shape, we call this new life cycle for innovation "The Shark Fin".

THE SHARK FIN

The Singularity
The Big Bang
The Big Crunch
Entropy

A list that deserves your attention

According to the Singularity University, these are the sectors that are currently still in the singularity phase, but from which a Zoonotic break-out is most likely in the years ahead:

1. Artificial intelligence (AI) and robotics
2. Augmented and virtual reality
3. Synthetic biology
4. Energy and environmental systems
5. Medicine and neuroscience
6. Nanotechnology and digital fabrication
7. Networks and computing systems
8. Policy, law, and ethics
9. Finance and economics
10. Synthesis and convergence
11. Entrepreneurship
12. Corporate innovation
13. Exponential organisations
14. Education

EXPERT OPINION

Omar Mohout

Entrepreneurship Fellow at Sirris

Predictive lists in a broader perspective

'No one can predict the future, but we can at least be certain of a number of matters: that things will be different; that these things will be rooted in the here and now; and that technology will be the lever for change and progress.

But every lever needs an Archimedes to set it in motion. It requires no more than a single person to start a revolution. However, this person must have a vision that looks much further than others and is so radical that at first very few people will share the same conviction. Then comes the eureka moment, a moment of singularity, when the idea is finally unfolded. Every fibre in your body will recognise this moment instantly and for a brief second you will find yourself standing beyond time and space. It is like hearing an entire piece of the most wonderful music compressed into the blink of an eye. Nothing is more powerful than an idea whose moment has come. But until that moment arrives and success is finally within your grasp, it is first necessary, often for some years, to swim against the stream until you eventually reach the source. It is this that allows you to initiate something totally new and radically different.

Since corona, we know that if a virus wants to be 'successful', it needs an incubation period and a reproduction number (R) that is greater than 1.

In other words, to develop a successful viral business, it is first necessary to work hard for decades, often in difficult circumstances, which can be economic (financing your venture), social (everyone thinks you are mad), physical (long and tiring days) and spiritual (what on earth are we doing?) in nature.

When you are finally ready to launch your Zoonotic idea, the customers who use your product or service must not only continue to come back time after time, but must also serve as ambassadors for your brand. In NPS (Net Promoter Score) terms, this means a score of 9 or 10. A constant influx of new customers combined with a higher retention of existing customers is the growth formula behind every Zoonotic. But you will also need investors who are prepared to lend you tons of cash to get you through the incubation period. And in a connected world in which winners expect to take the whole cake, growth at the cost of profits is another of the key unwritten rules. This explains the huge valuations for the Teslas, Amazons and Ubers, even though they are all still losing money hand over fist.

There are plenty of lists that attempt to predict the technology domains in which the next quantum leap will occur and where levers for change will become available. The most extreme of these are unquestionably the goal of achieving immortality, developing brain superpowers, creating artificial intelligence that is superior to human intelligence, or even the integration of man and machine.

But these lists are just that: someone's opinion of what might happen.

For the time being, there is no such thing as a time machine. The best way to predict the future is to try and shape it. It is a truism that everything that has ever existed will finally come to an end. We need to accept our own mortality and realise just how precious the time we still have really is. This realisation must lead to self-reflection about what we wish to achieve. How do we want to invest our remaining years? What impact do we hope to make? 'Death is the destination we all share,' said Steve Jobs in his speech at Stanford University. 'No one has ever escaped it. And this is how it should be, because death is very likely the single best invention of life. It is life's change agent.' Death is indeed the only certainty we humans have. Consequently, death reminds us that our time is limited. As soon as we become aware of this single, simple and unmistakeable fact, often as a result of something dramatic happening in our life, we no longer wish to waste something that we now realise is so precious. This forces us to look at the future in a new light and to identify the important changes we wish to accomplish.

You do not become a Zoonotic by chance. You become a Zoonotic through a conscious choice that has far-reaching consequences for yourself and for those around you.

This book is an excellent guide for those who dare to let the genie out of the bottle and will help you to prepare for what lies ahead. Because ideas have no value until they are shared or implemented.'

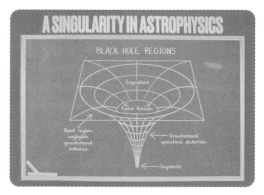

According to *Time Magazine*, people in the in tech world talk of singularity as the moment when machine power will eventually exceed the brain power of all the world's people combined. They predict that this will happen in 2045. When that moment arrives, people will be integrated with machines and become super-intelligent cyborgs. Exactly what this will look like (or rather what we will look like) is still very much of a black hole. The competition between humans and computers began when Deep Blue, a chess computer developed by IBM, beat the reigning world chess champion, Garry Kasparov, in 1996. Since then, the computing power of computers has increased exponentially, in accordance with Moore's Law, so that the power of artificial intelligence has increased by the same order.

As we approach singularity, the analogue and digital worlds will increasingly converge. This vision corresponds with the future predicted by Yuval Noah Harari for what he calls Homo Deus, a creature that will be superior to Homo Sapiens. Just think about the possibilities that this will offer to brands for connecting with customers in new ways. Too futuristic? Think again.

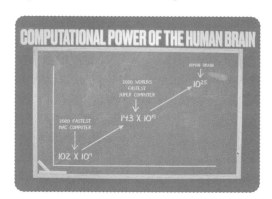

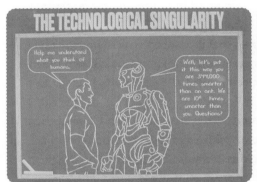

The aim of the Singularity University (https://su.org) is to support and accelerate the singularity process. It is a worldwide learning and innovation community, which makes use of exponential technologies to tackle the major challenges facing mankind, thereby helping to build a better world. Their collaborative platform offers everyone (irrespective of nationality) the opportunity to learn, share and connect, hoping in this way to speed up the breakthrough of innovative technologies such as artificial intelligence, robotics and digital biology. To make this possible, they offer various top-level (and fairly expensive) training courses and seminars. Their partners and participants are entrepreneurs, companies, non-profit organisations, government authorities, investors and academic institutions in more than 127 countries.

AI will change the face of health care

In the United States diabetes is the main cause of blindness. However, it seems that ophthalmologists only agree with the diagnoses of their colleagues in 60 percent of cases after viewing a retina scan. Worse still, they only agree with their own diagnosis in 65 percent of cases, if shown the same retina scan a second time. This is what Andrew Conrad of Verily told me during one of my study trips to the US. These are anomalies that can easily be eliminated through the use of AI. And not just in America. In India, for example, there is already a shortfall of more than 100,000 eye specialists. Google has developed a camera that can take photographs of your eye, which you can then send to the cloud, where you will receive a correct diagnosis and the right corrective therapy. New AI systems will also make it possible to follow up the collection and use of prescribed medication, since it appears that in 18 percent of cases patients never bother to obtain their medication or, even if they do, fail to take it or take it incorrectly. These are just a few examples of the low-hanging fruit where an AI Zoonotic could make a huge difference very quickly. It doesn't take a genius to work out what this could mean in terms of benefits for people's health. Once again, it is to be expected that a period of denial and resistance will first need to be overcome, but once this has happened the breakthrough will be able to expand and accelerate at speed.

Cake: a dormant Zoonotic in the financial sector?

The clever thing about a Zoonotic is the way that its unobtrusive existence initially allows it to avoid attention. But as soon as it reaches exponential growth speed, thanks to the support of the right influencers, it becomes impossible to stop.

I suspect, for example, that there are a number of currently dormant Zoonotics in the financial sector, which will make life very difficult for the traditional banks in the years ahead. In particular, I am looking towards China, the country that is currently the world leader in fintech and, more specifically, in payment systems, a field in which the Chinese are involved in a tech race with the United States. Through an aggressive approach, China has succeeded in developing a number of dominant and highly user-friendly payment platforms, such as the Alibaba Group's Alipay and Tencent's WeChat. These companies have quickly understood that you can transform the financial world through the use of AI to mine and exploit the mass of data contained in payment traffic. As a result, China is now in a position to export these dominant payment methods to the rest of the world, because elsewhere very few innovations have taken place in the financial sector in recent decades. The lever for these Chinese solutions is the fact that they are simple, easy and pleasant to use, which explains why they were able to spread so quickly in China. It is important to realise that although the majority of people are now online, e-commerce still only represents just 10 percent of all financial transactions. In other words, the online transfer of funds offers huge possibilities for rapid growth.

In our part of the world, one project waiting to benefit from this situation is Cake, an idea from the Limburg entrepreneur Davy Kestens, who first achieved fame with Sparkcentral. Cake is an app with which Kestens hopes to turn the current way of banking on its head. Commenting on Cake, the website of Spaargids.be wrote: 'Most people do not have a clear idea about the products and services on which they spend their wages. In most cases, they can only make rough estimates. But the independent banking app Cake looks set to change all that. Cake groups together all income and expenditure in a detailed summary. The figures can be looked at in different ways. By expenditure categories, such as restaurants, clothing, weekly domestic purchases, etc. Or by the accounts from which payments are made. Or in a globalised report that combines all your accounts in different banks. What's more, there is no need for you to change banks or open new accounts. You can link your existing accounts to Cake.

In addition to a summary of your own financial flows, in the future it will be possible to get a summary of groups of Cake users who have a similar profile to your own. This will allow you to compare the things on which you spend more or less than others. For this purpose, the app makes use of the new European PSD2 payment guideline. This offers consumers the possibility to give their permission to a third party for the collection and analysis of their transactions with various banks.

Apart from a summary of all your income and expenditure, Cake also offers its customers a nice extra. The users of the app can also earn money from it! For an average user this varies between 5 and 10 euros per month. The customer receives a partial refund of the purchase price of any purchase he/she makes from one of Cake's partners. And he/she receives a fee for allowing the use of his/her data. Cake then uses the transaction data of all its customers anonymously to compile group summaries. In turn, these summaries provide useful information about which goods and services are being bought by which groups of people, where, when and for how much. This information is valuable for sellers and manufacturers. Instead of carrying out expensive market research of their own, they can buy the same details at a much cheaper price from Cake, which also allows its customers to profit in part from the sale. Purely personal information is never shared by Cake with any third parties.'

INS**I**GHT

> **Fintech: a playground for potential Zoonotics**

The financial sector is unquestionably a prime area where all kinds of innovative applications will have a huge impact in the coming years. And I am not just thinking about the influence of Bitcoin and other similar ventures. Worldwide there are currently millions of immigrants and refugees without papers, which means that they cannot open a bank account. The Passbook app by Remity, a neo-bank, offers a solution for this large target group. Originally, Remity was only used to transfer money coming from their homeland. Now the system offers the possibility to open a proper bank account in the United States, without the need for the account holder to have a valid US social security number. A foreign passport or identity card with a photograph is sufficient. This opens up a whole new range of options for the world's 1.9 billion 'bankless' citizens.

Shazam lay slumbering for six years

In 1999, Philip Inghelbrecht from West Flanders and his friend Chris Barton, both then students at the University of California, thought that it might be useful if there was a way to quickly find out the name and the artist of any piece of music you heard by chance on the radio. In 2002, together with their friends Dhiraj Mukherjee, who worked for an internet consulting firm in London, and Avery Wang, who was studying at the University of Stanford, they launched the first paying application of their idea under the name 2580. This was the short number that you needed to dial on your (then not-so-smart) mobile phone to access the app. It was enough simply to send through a brief ten second excerpt of the song you were interested in, using the microphone of your GSM. A short while later, you would receive an SMS telling you the title of the song and the name of the singer. (For my younger readers this might sound like a story from the Middle Ages, whereas in fact it dates to less than two decades ago!) In 2004, the service was launched in the US, but the real breakthrough came in 2008, when they developed a new app for the iPhone with a link to iTunes. In 2011, it was the fourth most downloaded app in the App Store. This new version not only recognises the song or music, but immediately allows you to buy it from iTunes and shows you both the lyrics and the artwork of the relevant album. As a later addition, the app can now also recognise TV shows and even commercial adverts.

The graphic below demonstrates the rapid growth from zero in 2008 to 750 million users in 2015. Currently, there are well over 100 million people who use the app each month. It is clear that the iPhone in combination with iTunes was the Superspreader for Shazam. After the Zoonotic had lain slumbering for a period of six years (from 2002 to 2008), it took off like a rocket, eventually prompting Apple to offer 400 million dollars for its purchase in 2018. For them, it is the perfect way to attract customers for their pay-for-play music streaming service. That is the threat posed by the strength of the monster platforms like Facebook, Apple, Google and Amazon, whose deep pockets mean that they can sweep up most of the Zoonotics almost as soon as they emerge.

THE NUMBERS BEHIND MUSIC RECOGNITION APP SHAZAM
NUMBER OF SHAZAM USERS WORLDWIDE*

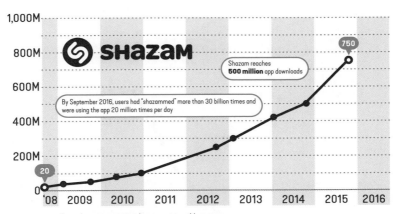

* numbers represent total users, not monthly active users;
Shazam hasn't disclosed new figures since October 2015

Source: Shazam

But don't forget that things can change very quickly in the Zoonotic world. Even as I write this, Google has just announced that it is offering a fun new application via its Google Search widget: sing, whistle or hum a song and Google will find the original for you and let you listen to it. The algorithm has been constructed in such a way that it reduces the melody to its essential elements, so that it doesn't matter if your singing, whistling or humming is not fully in tune. This extra service, offered by a Superspreader like Google, will inevitably force Apple Shazam to respond. That is the fate of every Zoonotic, performing an endless dance in which they challenge each other to continually evolve and improve, in much the same way that biological viruses also mutate and evolve over time. This, of course, is what we now know (to our cost) about corona, which is capable of mutating into more powerful, more infectious and more deadly variants at great speed.

Perlego: a Spotify for textbooks?

As most of you probably know from your own experience, textbooks take a serious bite out of the budget of every school-goer and student. Even more so if you know that the price of these books has risen much more dramatically than average consumer prices, as is clear to see from the diagram below.

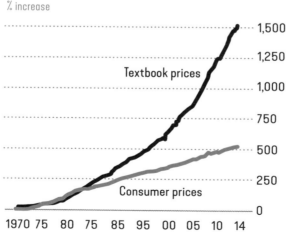

A TEXTBOOK CASE OF PRICE-GOUGING

% increase

Textbook prices

Consumer prices

1,500
1,250
1,000
750
500
250
0

1970 75 80 75 85 95 00 05 10 14

Source: Bureau of Labour Statistics

What if you didn't need to buy all those textbooks in one go, but instead could consult them online, whenever you need them? Or to put it another way: what if the Spotify business model could be applied to the textbook sector? That was the question that gave the Belgian entrepreneur Gauthier Van Malderen his idea for Perlego. The company, now established in London, with the Belgian Thomas Leysen (Umicore and Mediahuis) as one of its key investors, is now successfully putting this idea into practice.

Perlego offers you the freedom to consult textbooks 'in the cloud'. It has a range of more than 300,000 e-books from more than 2,300 different publishers. Moreover, the service is cross-device – it can be accessed via the web or iOS or Android apps – and is available in several languages. In addition to publishers from the United Kingdom, publishers from Germany, Scandinavia and Italy are also taking part. A subscription costs £12 per month. The big advantage for students is that they don't need to cough up a huge sum all at once at the beginning of each new term or academic year. They can be certain that the books they require will be available to them when and where they require them, and all without the need to take endless photocopies to keep in their files for revision purposes. The system also allows you to brainstorm with other students who have already read the book or a part of it. In this way, studying becomes a social activity, making it possible to pass on and receive tips and advice from fellow students all over the world.

Just like the music publishers before them with Spotify, book publishers now realise that they will lose some money because of Perlego, but at least in return it will reduce the impact of illegal pirating, the secondhand market and mass photocopying. The fact that some of the financial institutions in the UK that provide student loans now include a free Perlego subscription as part of their offer serves as a useful extra Superspreader, but one that also makes the banks potentially more attractive for first-time account openers. If banks offer free access to football results to attract young customers, why not also offer them free access to study material?

Perlego is another great example of how a Zoonotic works: two existing services – the library and e-textbook – combining to make use of the cloud as a Superspreader, with Perlego as the resulting new service that looks set to conquer the world with Cheetah-like speed. Perhaps in these circumstances it is hardly surprising that Northzone, the fund that led the very first capital round in Spotify, is now also investing in Perlego.

Strava: cycling and running together across time and place?

Strava – the Swedish word for 'striving' – was the brainchild of Mark Gainey and Michael Horvath back in 2009. Sportsmen and women use the app to share their routes and their times with other people in their social network. This makes it possible, if they so wish, to challenge and compete with each other. This adds an extra social dimension to cycling, running or walking. For example, I can run the same course as my friends at a totally different time, but we can still compare results. The San Francisco-based company currently has some 70 million users and is searching for capital that will allow it to achieve a stock market value of 1 billion dollars (making it a so-called 'unicorn'). Its business received a huge boost because of the corona crisis, which saw more and more people exercising out of doors during lockdown. Strava is now attempting to persuade these new users to switch to the paid version. This is a tried-and-tested Zoonotic strategy: first get your users hooked with a free version and then offer them a paying upgrade. Of course, the Strava app also collects mountains of data that can be useful for town planners; for example, to know where there is still a need for new cycle paths or to monitor the routes followed by commuters.

ONE MORE THING

EXPLORE UNKNOWN TRAILS

Strava, as the name suggests, is above all a performance-based app (speed, distance, time, etc.). For some people, this is a double-edged sword. In the words of one user: 'After a while, I was concentrating more on my time than on where I was running.' The rival Komoot app focuses on allowing its users to enjoy nature by helping them to explore new and unknown pathways. 'We love Tech. We love Nature. We make it easy for everyone to explore the world's most beautiful places.' That is how Komoot (the name means 'commute' in English) likes to present itself. The app was launched in 2014 by six young Berliners with the aim of making nature more accessible for hikers and cyclists. Its 10 million users can draw up their own routes, discovering new highways and byways that they can then share with others. They upload photos of whatever they pass along the way: ruins, temples, lakes, woods, mud pools and a thousand and one other things. In this way, these users serve as pioneers, which entitles them to a special status on Komoot.

AI and algorithms as a slumbering Zoonotic

Some economists are warning of the danger that algorithms – silently and stealthily – are gaining an ever-increasing stranglehold over the economy. They fear that AI systems that are programmed for maximum profit may have a serious negative effect on price setting, because the systems will eventually start to agree prices amongst themselves. This kind of conspiracy will be less easy to track down than more classic price-fixing arrangements – which are usually uncovered as a result of communication between the companies involved – because this new 'collusion' will be buried deep in the heart of super-complex algorithms.

The Zoonotic impact of this kind of automatic algorithm has already made itself tangibly felt in the so-called 'Flash Crash' on Wall Street in 2010, when the market lost 1 trillion dollars worth of value in just a matter of seconds through the action of algorithm-based automatic traders. In some sectors, such as the air industry, algorithms have been used for quite some time to determine flexible price setting. However, this happens on the basis of agreed rules that are set by the relevant programmers. But when use is made of AI and self-learning algorithms that are also able to communicate with each other, this 'safety net' falls away, resulting in a completely different ball game. In the online market, the prices of all your competitors are immediately available in real time. As a result, Amazon and Walmart, for example, are engaged in a never-ending bot war, in which prices are continually and automatically compared, assessed and undercut. Researchers in Germany have established that automatic systems have already concluded 'secret' price deals for, amongst other things, the retailing of petroleum.

In this respect, algorithms in combination with AI are a slumbering Zoonotic in almost every sector, the likely impact of which is at this stage incalculable. And don't think that it can't possibly happen to you. Remember the words of James Bond: 'Never say never'. You need to reflect seriously on the possible consequences for you and your company – because they could be serious.

In recent decades, a number of important evolutions have taken place. Whereas initially the internet was an open and decentralised network accessible to everyone, over the years a new and more centralised layer has been superimposed. With the emergence of AI, machine learning and cryptography, additional centralised layers will be created that will seek to identify people's intentions and preferences, information that is extremely valuable for the users. A telling example of this is Google Duplex.

Google Duplex

In this project, Google combines all its know-how in the fields of natural speech recognition, text-to-speech and deep learning. The system is already operational in the United States. On YouTube you can watch a demo in which the Google Assistant conducts a live telephone call with a hairdresser to book an appointment. Personally, I found the enthusiastic applause with which the spectators greeted this demo a little bit creepy: people applauding an application that makes people unnecessary... On the other hand, it is impossible to deny that this kind of digital butler can be handy for people like me, who need to wrestle with an over-packed agenda day after day. Some of the most obvious (and most useful) applications include:

1. In the home: what is the weather forecast for today?
2. In the car: where can I find a parking space?
3. My smartphone: send a message to my mother.
4. The possibility for people who cannot type to conduct searches and send messages by voice command alone.

No doubt in the future Google will also be able to book a hotel room or a car for me before I have even thought of it myself.

Airbnb takes the hotel sector out of its comfort zone

I believe that in the course of 2021 Airbnb will become the most valuable hotel and hospitality company in the world, as well as becoming one of the top-10 strongest global brands. Airbnb Inc. operates an online marketplace for travel information and booking services. It offers accommodation, host families and other tourist services via websites and mobile applications. Airbnb caters for customers all over the world, having more than 7 million different locations on its books. These are figures that can make even Amazon drool with envy.

According to Bloomberg, Airbnb Inc. is not actually part of the hotel industry, but properly belongs to the communication and media industry. Airbnb does indeed think and act like a technology company, and it is precisely that which makes it such a disruptive Zoonotic player. This Unfair Advantage of Airbnb guarantees it an unparalleled and worldwide magnetic attraction for its powerful offer.

A glance at the graphics below is enough to understand that the growth of Airbnb is very clearly exponential. That was also the conclusion of a study published in the *International Journal of Hospitality*, which commented tellingly as follows:

> 'The results provide empirical evidence that Airbnb will disrupt the hotel business, and that the more Airbnb users are satisfied with their experience, the more likely it is that demand for hotel rooms will decrease. Hotel managers therefore need to be aware of the level of service and price offered by Airbnb and other sharing platforms in their market. Airbnb offers in their locality can no longer be ignored and should be considered when developing revenue management strategies!'

NEW YEAR'S PEAK ILLUSTRATES AIRBNB'S GROWING STATURE

Estimated number of guests staying at Airbnb listings worldwide on New Year's Eve

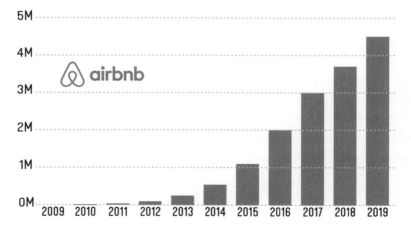

Source: *Airbnb*, Jon Erlichman

As already mentioned, a Zoonotic sometimes grows too aggressively, so that it incites seriously increased resistance. This is currently what is happening to Uber. The company has even been prohibited from operating in some countries, such as Spain and Thailand.

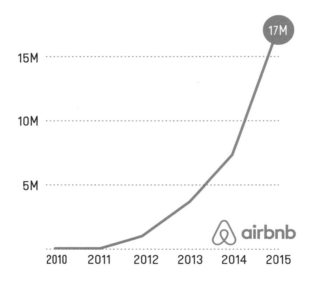

NUMBER OF GUESTS STAYING WITH AIRBNB
HOSTS DURING THE SUMMER

Source: Airbnb

Even though it was forced by the corona pandemic to dismiss a quarter of its 1,900 personnel in May 2020, Airbnb has still been able to retain its hero status, thanks to its empathic approach to this situation, which saw it offer generous termination bonuses, an extension of its staff medical cover, and the setting up of a website to help its former employees find new jobs.

ONE MORE THING

AIRBNB INCREASES ITS STOCK MARKET VALUE

While the travel sector in general has been hard hit by the corona crisis, Airbnb succeeded in finding an appropriate response to the situation that not only allowed it to limit the damage, but even – thanks to the perspective for effective vaccination – to increase its stock market value.

It was able to save money by cutting back on its staffing levels and by cancelling many planned new activities, including a series of flights and the setting up of its own TV studio. This, together with a smart refocusing on 'close-to-home' destinations, allowed Airbnb to stay more or less on track in 2020. By July, the number of bookings had returned to the same level as at the beginning of March: 1 million overnight stays worldwide. It was noticeable that half of these Airbnb tourists now travelled less than 500 kilometres to their destination. As a result, the summer quarter was one of the most profitable quarters in the company's entire history, resulting in gross net profits of 501.4 million dollars. On the first day of its stock market launch, its value immediately broke through the 85 billion barrier, significantly more than Expedia and about the same as Booking. com.

With the above examples, I want to make it clear that no sector is safe from a Zoonotic. So don't think it can never happen to you. You need to devise a Zoonotic strategy and you need to devise it NOW! The Zoonotic that threatens your company won't necessarily come from your own sector, but will often come from a completely different industry. Zoonotics are appearing faster and faster all the time, and they just keep on coming, in part as a result of increasing globalisation. Just because you cannot see a Zoonotic now, this does not mean that one isn't lurking just round the corner. And even when you realise that a Zoonotic is heading your way, it will still strike you more quickly than you ever imagined possible. Your only hope? Be prepared!

3

A ZOONOTIC ACCELERATES EXPONENTIALLY

One of the characteristics of a Zoonotic is the Cheetah-like speed with which it surprises friend and foe alike. This acceleration begins deceptively slowly, but then picks up pace at an astonishing rate. Or as Ernest Hemingway replied, when asked how he became bankrupt: 'Gradually. Then suddenly.' But don't confuse a Zoonotic with a trend or a hype. A real Zoonotic is here to stay.

Much faster than a trend

As a result of increased digitalisation, today's trends are more likely to spread more quickly than in the past. For example, one well-known economic long-term trend is the Kondratiev curve, named after the Russian economist Nikolai Kondratiev, who discovered that capitalist economies progress in a series of wave-like movements. A period of high growth is inevitably followed by a period of low growth, after which a new upwards surge will start. Kondratiev calculated that an economic cycle lasts for approximately 50 years (25 years up and 25 years down).

In Belgium, this curve came into prominence thanks to the work of the Ghent professor Helmut Gaus, who linked it to his study of human behaviour during the alternating periods of growth and decline. On the occasion of his departure from the university in 2010, Gaus said in the magazine *Trends* that, following the economic nadir that had been reached in 1990, the situation had been improving ever since and would reach a new peak around 2021. But who could have predicted that by that date the world would be in the grip of a disruptive pandemic that upset everyone's calculations and took us all – trend watchers included – by surprise? This proves yet again that a Zoonotic is capable of turning expected trends – which tend to be linear – on their head.

You don't need to read the excellent book *Factfulness* by the late lamented Hans Rosling to realise that the human brain is not very good when it comes to interpreting facts and predicting the future. According to Rosling: 'Even those who have access to the most up-to-date sources sometimes make the wrong call.' The truth of this statement has been proven repeatedly during the corona crisis by the widely varying opinions of the many experts about the measures that need to be taken, without even considering the confused bleatings of the twittering masses on social media.

To my mind, there are five key trends that I regard as forming a crucial undercurrent in today's society.

1. **Diversity and inclusion**, not only in terms of age, gender and race, but also in terms of knowledge. For this reason, diversity in background is equally important. Does everyone have the same knowledge? Or do some people have different knowledge? An older person with an academic background, viewing history, might see that dealing with problems often takes time and will approach such matters with patience. A younger person with a business background will be more inclined to think in terms of cycles of three months and will seek to find short-term solutions. Neither of these visions is necessarily worth more than the other. What we need is a mix of both. For example, half of the board of directors of the Port of Antwerp (of which I am a member) is made up of women. Additionally, we also have a wide range of different backgrounds.

2. **Purpose.** Companies must constantly question their position in the world and whether or not they are worthy of it. Will people miss them if they are no longer there? This is a strategically crucial issue. Today's generation, unlike their parents and grandparents, need to know why they are expected to get up at six o'clock each morning to go to work. The best way for companies to attract and keep staff in the modern economy is to have a clear purpose. You still need convincing about the persuasive power of purpose? Have a look at

the TED talk 'Start with Why' by Simon Sinek. Closely related to the question of purpose is the growing importance of company culture. This results in a new way of looking at the economy. Klaus Schwab, chairman of the World Economic Forum in Davos, describes this as 'Stakeholder Capitalism: a manifesto for a cohesive and sustainable world', which he sees as a worthwhile and viable alternative for the current dominant model of Shareholder Capitalism or State Capitalism (see https://www.weforum.org/press/ 2020/01/stakeholder-capitalism-a-manifesto-for-a-cohesive-and-sustainable-world/).

3. **Climate.** This is not exactly a new trend, but, thanks in part to the efforts of (amongst others) Youth for Climate, it is now more firmly on the social and political agenda than ever before.

4. **Activism.** Ordinary people are more assertive and more empowered than ever before. As a result of increasing digitalisation, they now have easy access to multiple channels for communicating their grievances. Think, for example, of the Yellow Jackets in France; the pro-democracy protests in Hong Kong; Brexit; climate marches; Black Lives Matter. These are all causes around which people can unite. And there are plenty of others. My parents' generation was briefly inspired in a similar way by the events of May 1968, but the momentum soon faded. Now you can see a much faster rhythm of successive waves of activism, which have a kind of domino effect on each other.

5. **The culture of sharing.** From car sharing to co-working via Wikipedia or digital platforms like Zoom and Microsoft Teams: all these initiatives prove that collaboration and the sharing of knowledge are becoming increasingly easier and more popular. In his bestseller *Sapiens*, Yuval Noah Harari argues that humans are the only primates that have succeeded in conquering the world, precisely because of their talent for working together with others outside their own immediate circle, a process that was further inspired in more recent times by shared stories in the form of religions, political convictions, role models, influencers and brands.

OBLIO DISINFECTS YOUR SMARTPHONE

It seems that there are something like 17,000 different bacteria on an average smartphone – which is more than you can find on an average toilet seat! Oblio looks like an elegant vase. You place your telephone inside it and it is not only 99 percent disinfected, but your battery is also automatically and wirelessly recharged. Why am I not surprised that this product was sold out almost as soon as it reached the stores? It is another classic example of two useful applications combined into one: the first golden rule for any successful Zoonotic.

A Zoonotic can make grateful use of some of the above mentioned trends to speed up its own success. For example, there is a clear link between our current environmental and climate problems and COVID-19. A recent article in *De Morgen* newspaper was tellingly titled: 'Less nature, more danger: how we roll out the red carpet for deadly viruses'. The article's author, Barbara Debusschere, went on to write: 'One out of every three infectious diseases, which are primarily transferred from animals, can be connected with the destruction of the tropical rain forests for mining, agriculture or urbanisation. This is the conclusion of a study by the Eco-Health Alliance, an American NGO that traces new viruses in wild animals.' So we had better prepare ourselves for worse to come. Because even when we have finally managed to tame corona, another new and super-fast Zoonotic will be waiting in the wings. According to Professor Dr Marc Buelens, dealing with the corona crisis is child's play when compared with what will be necessary to deal with the climate crisis. In other words, there will be many more tense and difficult years ahead.

More disruptive than a hype

A hype is a short-term phenomenon that often disappears as quickly as it arrived. It is like the sharp tip of a shark's fin that suddenly but briefly emerges above the waters of a longer trend wave. Think of things like Pokémon, Flippos, the Ice Bucket Challenge, etc. Nowadays, hypes of this kind follow each other more quickly than ever before, an acceleration made possible in part by the omnipresence of digital tools and aids.

Make sure you don't become a hype, because hypes never last for long. As a marketeer, avoid making rash promises when your sales team asks if you can think of something to help them meet their short-term targets or when management asks if you can come up with a film that will go viral. Make sure, of course, that you remain a constructive partner for your colleagues, but do not be afraid to temper their enthusiasm. Never put yourself out on a limb, but maintain your proper position between the company and its customers. When I worked for Proximus, I made frequent use of the figures from previous marketing campaigns and of tried and tested frameworks. This helped to create trust and allowed me to develop realistic marketing projects in collaboration with other internal stakeholders.

The diagram below shows how disruptive companies distinguish themselves from classic companies in every phase of the value chain.

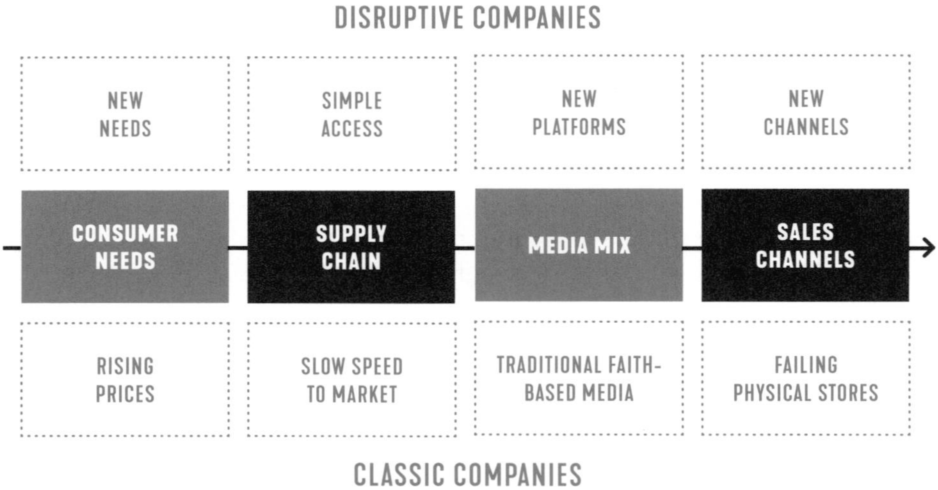

DISRUPTIVE COMPANIES

NEW NEEDS	SIMPLE ACCESS	NEW PLATFORMS	NEW CHANNELS
CONSUMER NEEDS	**SUPPLY CHAIN**	**MEDIA MIX**	**SALES CHANNELS**
RISING PRICES	SLOW SPEED TO MARKET	TRADITIONAL FAITH-BASED MEDIA	FAILING PHYSICAL STORES

CLASSIC COMPANIES

Exponential growth: a Cheetah at top speed

Experience has repeatedly shown that our human brain is primarily good for linear and local thinking, but much less suited to exponential thinking. In the summer of 2020, when the experts warned us of the imminent approach of a second wave of corona infections, it seemed as if the world's policy makers found it difficult to grasp the true extent of the danger. The water has not yet reached our lips, they told us... The crowds of lockdown shoppers in city centres similarly illustrated how difficult it is for many ordinary people to understand just how fast and how powerful a Zoonotic really is. A comment I read on Facebook made this same point amusingly but tellingly: 'The virologists have succeeded in convincing 80 percent of people of the danger. It is now up to the vets to convince the remaining 20 percent.' That says a lot about the human race.

In the digital world, change nearly always takes place at an exponential rate of growth. Perhaps the most well-known example of this is Moore's Law, named after Gordon Moore, one of the founders of the microchip manufacturer Intel. His law predicted that the number of transistors in a computer chip – and therefore its computing speed – would double roughly every two years. And his prediction came true, as the graphic below demonstrates. Whereas in 1962 there were just nine transistors in a microchip, by 2010 this number had rise to two billion.

MOORE'S LAW

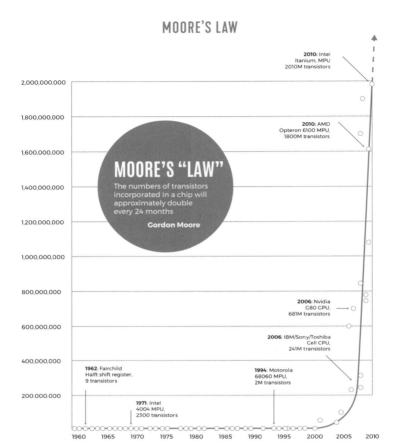

'Technological change is exponential, contrary to the common-sense "intuitive linear" view. So we won't experience 100 years of progress in the 21st century – it will be more like 20,000 years of progress.'

RAY KURZWEIL
CO-FOUNDER SINGULARITY UNIVERSITY

Another striking example to explain how exponential growth works is the legend told in India about the inventor of the chess board. Wikipedia describes this legend as follows: 'According to tradition, the game of chess was invented about 1,500 years ago by Sissa, a wise man from India. He subsequently taught the king to play the game. The king was so enthusiastic that he decided that chess should serve as an example for all his people, since it had shown him that the peasants (the pawns) and the nobles (the other pieces) must work together to achieve victory.

The king promised Sissa a reward for his invention, a reward that he was free to choose. The wise man asked for one grain of rice (or wheat, depending on the version of the story) to be placed on the first square of the chessboard, two grains on the second square, four grains on the third square, eight grains on the fourth square and so on. The number of grains would be doubled on each successive square, until all sixty-four squares had been filled.

At first, the king felt insulted, because Sissa had asked him for what seemed to be such a modest reward. But he soon changed his mind when the officials of his treasury told him just how many grains of rice this would mean: in total, more than 18 trillion (a number with 20 digits!) grains would be needed, which was many times more than the world's entire production each year...' Impressive, isn't it? And that is exactly the way a Zoonotic works.

Take the test yourself

Ask a colleague or a member of your family the following question: If I give you 1 euro today and if I double that amount every day for a whole month, how many euros do you think you will have at the end of the 31 days? What do you think? For the mathematically inclined, you can use the following formula: the total amount is equivalent to 1×2^t, where t is equal to 31, the number of days in a full month. For the rest of us (who can't be bothered to work it out), the answer is 2,147,483,648 euros!

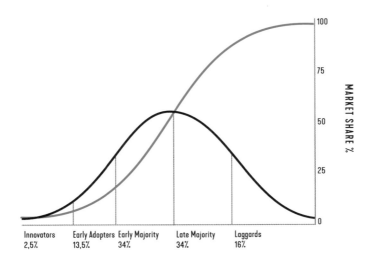

In their book *ConneXion*, Jan De Schepper and Paul Van Den Bosch write: 'One of the most underrated "new" challenges for the leader is dealing with exponential thinking.' According to them, this will result in three frequently occurring mental and emotional sensations:

1. **Cognitive dissonance**
   What happens is so far outside our known frames of reference and known patterns of behaviour that we have a tendency to deny the reality of the situation.
2. **Confusion**
   There is chaos inside our head. We temporarily no longer know what we should do. We have lost direction.
3. **Disengagement**
   We feel discouraged and have a tendency to withdraw from the situation.

These are all sensations that a Zoonotic can use or abuse to pursue its conquest of the world.

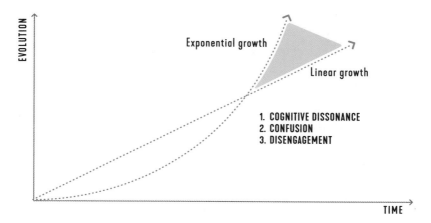

EXPONENTIAL THINKING LEADS TO HUMAN DISCOMFORT

Source: *ConneXion*, Jan De Schepper and Paul Van Den Bosch

Attempting to achieve exponential growth is important if you wish to build up a strategic lead over your possible competitors. Uber, for example, knew right from the very start that it was necessary to build up a network of drivers and customers very quickly, even if that meant the company making a loss for a number of years. It is that network that now represents their competitive advantage, not their app, since the latter can easily be copied.

'In my Belgian homeland, I often experience a kind of 'that's-not-how-we-do-it-here' culture. You find much less of that in California.' So says Bart Decrem, the Belgian entrepreneur who runs the start-up incubator for Mozilla in the book *The Secret of of Silicon Valley*. 'Here you have a stronger sense of freedom. You don't need anyone's permission to try something new. The starting point is "yes" and everyone works in top gear. In Belgium the starting point is "no" and everyone remains stuck in first gear.'

The reproductive factor determines the speed of growth

During the corona crisis, the virologists were constantly talking about the reproduction factor of the virus, which was known as the R-factor. This number indicates how many other people are infected by a single infected person. If the R-factor is 1, the infected person will infect one other person, so that the evolution of the virus is linear. If the R-factor is less than 1, this is a signal that infection rates are falling. If the R-factor is higher than 1, this means that the pandemic is increasing in strength and will soon start to snowball. Measles, for example, is highly infectious and has an R-factor of 15 in a community that has not been inoculated against it. With corona (officially SARS-CoV-2), the reproduction rate in the absence of protection is 3. During the peak of the pandemic in 2020 the highest R-factor was 2.3. In other words, since the R-factor was higher than 1, the door was open for an exponential growth of infection, as illustrated in the diagrams below.

R RATE OF 1

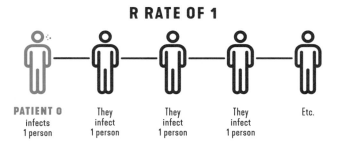

| PATIENT 0 infects 1 person | They infect 1 person | They infect 1 person | They infect 1 person | Etc. |

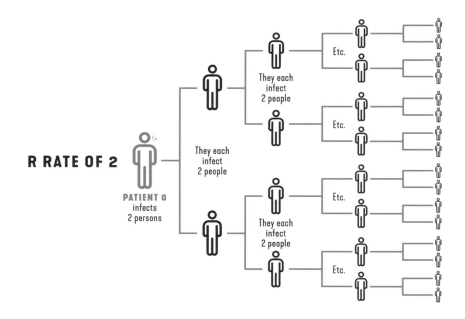

R RATE OF 2

The following graphic illustrates how quickly an effective strategy is able to slow down and reduce the R-factor.

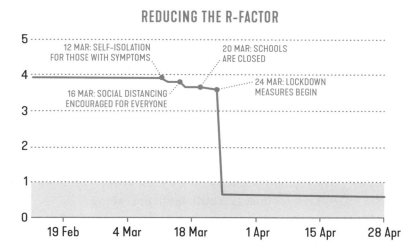

REDUCING THE R-FACTOR

The R-factor is also important for the evolution of your viral business strategy. An R-factor less than 1 means that every customer or user encourages less than one other person to buy your product or service. Your viral strategy will only be successful if your R-factor is greater than 1. Or to express it in terms of my Unfair Advantage metaphor: the R-factor symbolises the speed with which the Cheetah conquers the savannah.

On the one hand, the reproductive power of your business strategy is dependent on reciprocity; namely, the extent to which one user of your product also encourages others to use it. On the other hand, it is also dependent on the network effect; namely, the extent to which the user of your product can gain benefit from encouraging other people from his/her network to also use it. This latter factor increases the motivation of existing users to 'infect' others. In this way, a relatively minor player in the US telecom market was able to rapidly increase its market share with a Friends & Family tariff plan. If you could convince your friends or members of your family to also become a customer of the operator in question, both parties were given a preferential tariff for their telephone conversations with each other. In other words, the operator compensated for its small size by making clever use of the networks of its customers.

You can do this exercise for yourself. Try to recall who was the first person to put you in contact with WhatsApp. Then try to recall how many people you in turn encouraged to make use of this quick and easy way of communicating within the various 'groups' to which you belong (colleagues, parents, school, family, sports club, etc.).

Who or what persuaded you to buy your first mobilephone? Originally, this device was primarily intended (because of its large battery and equally large aerial) as a car phone for businessmen and professionals, but word of mouth soon saw it break into the private sphere. Nowadays, it is almost a ritual that every young person gets a smartphone for their 12th birthday (if not before).

A good influencer strategy has an important impact on the growth speed of your Zoonotic strategy. However, it is crucial not to use your influencers as 'one-shot wonders'. You need to build up a long-term relationship with them. Ask yourself (and find answers for) the following questions:
  - What kind of influencer is most suitable for your company?
  - How can you build up a long-term relationship with them?
  - If you are a founder or a CEO, can you be an influencer for your own company?

You can only calculate your R-factor retrospectively, by using the following parameters:

1. **Susceptible:** These are all the customers who might switch their allegiance to your Zoonotic competitor. Initially, this might mean your entire customer portfolio, because you do not yet have sufficient information to segment them more appropriately.
2. **Exposed:** This is the group that is most subject to the efforts of your competitor to win them over and are therefore most likely to desert your company, although they have not yet given any indication of doing so.
3. **Churned:** These are the customers that you have lost partially or completely to your competitor.
4. **Won back:** This is the group that you have been able to win back from your competitor and who (no longer) consciously opt for your rival.

The R-value is a number that evolves through time. It is important not only if you are trying to develop your own Zoonotic strategy, but also when you are subjected to an attack by a hostile Zoonotic.

A Zoonotic can mutate

Its ability to mutate makes a Zoonotic extra dangerous. In a business context this means that, even if you are already a Zoonotic, this does not release you from the obligation to continue improving and innovating. In this sense, a Zoonotic fits perfectly into the Darwinian evolutionary model, since it constantly reinvents itself, so that it can keep growing. Consider, for example, how a successful company like Facebook has developed numerous new applications over the years, including Messenger (as a response to the SMS), video (as a response to YouTube) and Stories (as a response to Instagram).

Growth is fine, but never lose sight of your customers

Robinhood Markets Inc. in California has developed a new app that makes it possible with just a few simple swipes of your smartphone to trade in shares, stock options and cryptocurrencies, using either your fingerprint or facial recognition to ensure the security of the transactions. Robinhood works exclusively online, does not have an office and does not charge commission. They earn their income from the interest on the cash account of their customers and by selling information to high-frequency day traders.

Thanks to the app's ease of use, the number of customers skyrocketed in 2020 to more than 13 million. In spring of that year alone an additional 3 million customers were attracted, which had harmful consequences for the stock market. As a result, for example, the rise in the value of Tesla shares ran exactly parallel with the growth in the number of Robinhood users. This meant that if you wanted to know what the Tesla shares were likely to do the next day, all you had to do was look at the number of new Robinhood customers. So far, so good. Unfortunately, in the autumn of 2020 a number of reports began to appear via Bloomberg which suggested that the app was not as safe as people had been led to believe and that the money of some investors had disappeared. Robinhood tried to deny responsibility, saying that the problem was not theirs: they confirmed that their systems were bug-free and had not been hacked. Not everyone was reassured and the fact that the company did not even have a telephone number where worried customers could voice their concerns made matters worse. Eventually, it became clear that the company had indeed been the victim of smart cyber-criminals, in the form of a supposedly rich Ethiopian prince, who was looking for a 'safe' way to secure his inheritance. It is clear that Robinhood was too eager to grow quickly and, consequently, failed to invest sufficiently in the security of its customers. It is ironic that they did so under the name of a sympathetic bandit like Robin Hood, who was famed for robbing the rich to give to the poor – and not the other way around...

Just like Uber, Robinhood is a Zoonotic that was too greedy for fast growth, so that it failed to take proper care of the interests and concerns of its customers. As a result, they have put their own future in jeopardy. This kind of Predatory Zoonotic is not what I wish to promote in this book. For me, respect for your customers and for certain ethical values are basic principles from which you should never deviate.

In the meantime, another challenger has now emerged, this time from China (where else?). It is called Webull and was set up by Alibaba (who else?). In just 12 months this online stockbroker has increased its portfolio of customers fourteen-fold to more than 2 million. True, this is still fairly modest in comparison with Robinhood's 12 million, but Webull plans to further expand its offer by introducing a robo-advice service, which will provide automatic financial and investment guidance. In other words, Robinhood needs to watch out. It is already unusual that a Chinese company like Webull is doing so well in the United States, at a time when the economic relations between the two countries are at an all-time low. But the American investors don't seem to care. They are more interested in Webull's user-friendliness and the fact that it gives supplementary (and valuable) financial tips. This means that Webull is even capable of competing with the services of the expensive high-end brokers, like the Interactive Broker Group. It will be interesting to see how this develops.

> **Who are the Robinhood customers?**

During the stock market crash initiated by the corona crisis, millions of new young investors worldwide opened an investment account. The greatest amount of interest was shown in the United States, where widespread use was made of online applications like Robinhood. The same trend can also be seen here in Belgium, according to the results of a survey carried out by Keytrade Bank amongst 1,000 of its investors. 'Many young people clearly saw the corona crisis as an opportunity to earn some extra cash. Almost one in ten Belgians younger than 35 years of age reported that they had invested more actively since the start of the corona crisis than they had done previously.' The majority of these investors focus on companies that have much in common with their own day-to-day lives, which are dominated by the rise of digital. Instead of watching TV, they now watch vlogs on YouTube or series and films on streaming platforms like Netflix and Disney+. As a result, they also invest in the shares of these companies and other similar ones, like Google and its mother, Alphabet.

Is Facebook a Predatory Zoonotic?

The aggressive 'buy or bury' strategy, with which Facebook systematically seeks to remove potential competitors, is coming under increasing pressure. Like Alphabet, the mother company of Google, Facebook is now under fire in a number of American states from the US Ministry of Justice. The concentration of power in these giant corporations is now seen as a potential threat for the proper functioning of the free market, which is one of the foundations of Western capitalism. In reality, Google and Facebook are indeed Predatory Zoonotics, though the difference between them is that Google tries to act like James Bond: a smooth and sympathetic gentleman, but a killer nonetheless. Together with the many other companies gathered under the umbrella of mother company Alphabet, Google likes to portray itself as serving society at large. Of course, I am not naive and I (like many others) realise that the main aim of these actions is to acquire even more data. Google further pretends that it is not (in contrast to Amazon) a threat to retailers. They claim that their Shopping Actions application, which makes it possible for customers to pay via the Google Payment platform, is actually intended to help retailers. Which perhaps it does, until these retailers one day discover that their customers are suddenly expecting much more from them.

Yet even a Predatory Zoonotic like Facebook is not immune from attack by another Zoonotic. This was evident, for example, during the commotion that arose after Facebook announced its decision to integrate all the data on WhatsApp into their global database without encryption. A single post from Elon Musk was enough to persuade 25 million users in just 72 hours to make the switch to the rival Telegram platform, which, apparently, deals with the privacy of its users more respectfully. To try to counteract this coup, Facebook even went so far (it is claimed) as to spread false information about Telegram, which suggests that the monopolist felt seriously threatened. Which is a good thing, as far as I am concerned. I think Telegram is more fun to use than WhatsApp, anyway. Of course, that is a purely anecdotal testimony and also statistically irrelevant, since N=1!

4

A ZOONOTIC KNOWS NO BOUNDARIES

In the corona world, a Superspreader is a person who infects many other people in a short space of time. In this respect, the barman at Ischgl in Austria has become famous (or, rather, notorious). At the start of February 2020, this man made world news when it was discovered that he had infected eleven people from four different countries with COVID-19. A short while later, it became known that a South Korean woman had probably infected no fewer than 37 members of her church community. In both cases, the authorities already used the term 'Superspreaders', because these patients had infected far more people than the average (which, according to research by the British Imperial College, is 2.6 people).

In the context of a viral business Zoonotic, the Superspreader is the distributor of the new product. In many cases, this distributor is now often the smartphone, although 'tools' like social media or Google can also be powerful Superspreaders. They all offer a wide range of low threshold, worldwide platforms that allow anyone and everyone, with just a minimal investment, to spread their message with Cheetah-like speed. However, the problem with this is that word 'everyone'. Not 'everyone' uses 'social' media with the best of intentions. This frequently leads to fraud and fake news, to such an extent that even Eric Schmidt, the former CEO of Google, was forced to concede during a *Wall Street Journal* conference that the company that he had helped to put on the world economic map could also have undesirable effects.

In Google's defence, he added that, in his opinion, so far no social media plat-form had yet succeeded in effectively eliminating or even stemming the tide of this kind of negative impact. This makes the situation more complicated and less certain for the average user. But even if many people are only asymptomatic carriers of stupidity, this does not absolve companies like Google, Facebook and Instagram from their responsibility in these matters.

> 'The context of social networks serving as amplifiers for idiots
> and crazy people is not what we intended.'
> **ERIC SCHMIDT**

In the run-up to the 2020 presidential election in the United States, the Mozilla Foundation – an organisation that seeks to preserve the internet as a public re-source, open and accessible to all – compiled a detailed comparative table to indi-cate how the different social media platforms dealt with fake news and other sim-ilar phenomena. The idea is that this table will be continually updated to monitor the changing policy of Facebook, Google, Instagram, YouTube, Twitter and Tik-Tok. It is a bold and praiseworthy initiative, but essentially a waste of time. Pearls before swine, if you like. Who is going to make the effort to consult a complex table of parameters that is constantly changing? Even so, I can still recommend a visit to their website https://foundation.mozilla.org. It is well worth a look.

INSIGHT

> ### › The power of the Superspreader

COVID-19 has taught us that on average an infected person further infects between two and four other people with the virus. In essence, the spread of the disease follows the Pareto Principle: a small group of roughly 20 percent is responsible for roughly 80 per-cent of the total number of infections. However, there is no good explanation for this distorted effect. Take, for example, the case of patient No. 31 from South Korea. The first 30 infections in that country were limited to her family and close friends. But No. 31, a 61-year-old woman, gave the epidemic a real push in the wrong direction by twice visit-ing her local church, during which she infected an estimated 15 other people. Not long after that, several thousand infections could be linked to those two church visits.

A Zoonotic uses the Superspreader to insidiously work its way closer to its target groups. If you use the services of a Zoonotic company like Zoom or Microsoft Teams, you provide unimpeded access to the other users you invite to participate in the session, thereby exposing them to possible infection as well. In this way, you ensure that the application comes into contact with more and more people. For the Zoonotic, this is a non-intrusive way to intrusively gain popularity.

Think global, act local

A biological Zoonotic makes grateful use of our increasingly globalised way of living: international trade offers it many ways to spread, with cargo ships, planes, high-speed trains and cruise ships as its favourite modes of transportation. A business Zoonotic makes use of the fact that the thinking of many companies is still much too linear and much too local. In addition to its exponential growth, it is crucial for the success of a Zoonotic that it thinks and works on a worldwide scale. This is one of its most deadly characteristics. The old adage of 'think local, act global' has now been replaced by 'think global, act local', a principle proven by many of the successful Zoonotic companies mentioned in earlier pages.

> A viral Zoonotic strategy must ensure that the Cheetah
> leaves the familiar territory of the savannah and sets its sights
> on the wider world.

Consider, for example, the case of Posios, the very first point-of-sale system on iPad for restaurants, developed by Zhong Xu and Jan Hollez. I met Zhong at a Leadership Meeting in Paris. His story is a typical example of a Zoonotic, which began its lonely journey in the savannah. He had no starting capital and had to mortgage his house to secure the loan he needed. Eventually, he managed to get a crucial foot in the door with important backers in Singapore and New York. They wanted to launch the app worldwide and, with this in mind, opened local offices almost everywhere. You can have the best product in the world, but it is worthless if people know nothing about it. But Zhong and his team had the right feeling: 'Let's go and conquer the world!' It sounds naive? Perhaps. But as an entrepreneur this is sometimes the confidence you need to have and the risk you need to take. And it worked! Posios came onto the radar of the American Lightspeed, one of the largest cloud-based software companies in the retail world. Their CFO telephoned Zhong personally and literally asked: 'You guys wanna marry us?' To which Zhong replied: 'Let's date first.' Both sides quickly came to the conclusion that this could be an excellent (and very profitable) synergy. What followed was a successful management buy-out and the opening of an important new chapter in Zhong's entrepreneurial career.

More Zoonotics are on the way

According to some biologists, there are tens of millions of as yet undiscovered viruses living in nature. The likelihood that they will develop into Zoonotics that can then be transferred to humans is getting bigger and bigger all the time, largely because of our modern way of life that puts nature under increasing pressure through over-population and the demands of a globalised economy with worldwide transport and distribution systems.

In a similar way, viral business strategies can profit from a number of important evolutions that increase their chances of spreading exponentially.

1. **The falling cost of creation and innovation**
   This includes, for example, the increasingly reduced cost of computer hardware, together with the exponential improvement in the performance of microchips and software. In combination with efficient supply chains, this makes it possible for Zoonotic players, both great and small, to challenge their competitors simultaneously in three strategically important areas: high-quality products and services at a lower price and with more options than ever before for made-to-measure personalisation.

2. **The falling cost of information**
   Through the explosion of social networks, with their host of bloggers, reviews, instruction videos and suchlike, consumers now have access to huge amounts of information on which to base their decisions. As a result, experimental products and services are picked up and spread more quickly than in the past, so that Zoonotics are now less dependent on a small group of early adopters.

3. The falling cost of experimentation

Because of today's hyper-connectivity, more and more people worldwide can easily collaborate and test out new ideas, while keeping the costs and the risks relatively limited. This means that new products and services can be assessed more quickly and more easily by potential customers.

4. Direct-to-consumer relations

Thanks to a viral Zoonotic business strategy, companies can now successfully cut out important links in the supply chain, allowing them to come into direct contact with the end-users, with increased shareholder value as an immediate consequence. Following globalisation and digitalisation, we are now entering the new age of Zoonotic dispersion.

Everything is becoming faster, smaller, cheaper, more powerful and more available. For this reason, the classic bell curve for the adoption of an innovation, as originally sketched by Rogers, looks totally different in a Zoonotic context.

BIG BANG MARKET ADOPTION

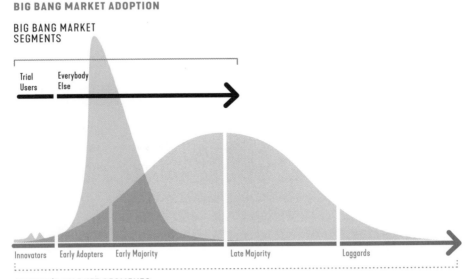

BIG BANG MARKET
SEGMENTS

Trial Users — Everybody Else

Innovators — Early Adopters — Early Majority — Late Majority — Laggards

ROGERS'S MARKET SEGMENTS

Source: *Accenture*

FULL METAL JACKET

Vollebak developed a bacteria-free raincoat, woven from no less than 11 kilometres of wafer-thin copper wire. This coat is not only resistant to bacteria, but is also windproof and waterproof, as well as being comfortable to wear, thanks to the fleece lining. The developers emphasise that copper, which was first formed billions of years ago by old supernovas, has always played a key role in important innovations: its ability to conduct heat and energy, its use in medical instruments and for the disinfection of water, to name but a few. Vollebak's ambition is evident from their mission statement: 'Vollebak aims to do for outdoor clothing what Tesla did for cars and El Bulli did for food, using science, wit and imagination to create products noremove hyphen, insert space no one thought possible.'

In his masterclass during the online event Media & Culture Fast Forward, Peter Hinssen warned that we would all be wise to prepare for a number of far-reaching seismic shocks in at least four different domains:

1. Technological seismic shocks
2. Ecological seismic shocks
3. Biological seismic shocks
4. Geopolitical seismic shocks

In the second part of the book, I will challenge you to pick up the gauntlet and start immediate work on developing a Zoonotic viral business strategy that will allow you not only to deal with these shocks but also to take advantage of them.

cheCKList

A ZOONOTIC COMBINES TWO EXISTING ELEMENTS
TO CREATE SOMETHING SURPRISINGLY NEW

THE BIRD
Unfair
Advantage 1

AND THE BAT
Unfair
Advantage 2

**ENSURE VIA
THE PIG**
Superspreader

THAT A NEW PRODUCT OR SERVICE (THE ZOONOTIC) CAN SPREAD AT AN EXPONENTIAL SPEED, LIKE A TRUE

CHEETAH

A ZOONOTIC FIRST SLUMBERS, BEFORE SUDDENLY BURSTING ONTO THE SCENE.

- IT STARTS WITH A SINGULARITY.
- THE BIG BANG SO CREATED DEVELOPS AN UNSTOPPABLE MOMENTUM.

A ZOONOTIC SPREADS AND GROWS EXPONENTIALLY.

- FASTER THAN A TREND
- MORE DISRUPTIVE THAN A HYPE
- THE R-FACTOR DETERMINES THE GROWTH POWER
- BEWARE THAT YOU DO NOT BECOME A PREDATOR ZOONOTIC

A ZOONOTIC KNOWS NO BOUNDARIES.

- THINK GLOBAL, ACT LOCAL.
- MORE ZOONOTICS IN YOUR SECTOR ARE ON THE WAY!

PART 2

HOW DO YOU BECOME A ZOONOTIC?

To develop your own successful viral Zoonotic business strategy, it is best to take your Unfair Advantage as your starting point. To set this process in motion, you will need a Zoonotic leader, someone who dares to question the status quo and has the courage to leave the familiar and comfortable pathways. You will also need the support of a Zoonotic team, a group of people with the right talents and, above all, an open and flexible mindset. Together, you must devise and implement a Zoonotic strategy. Based on the nature of your existing Unfair Advantage (spreader 1), go in search of a second Unfair Advantage (spreader 2), which you can combine to create something new (the Superspreader). This new proposition is your Zoonotic. Try to find something that meets a latent need. Remember to think not just locally, but also globally.

In his masterclass during the online event Media & Culture Fast Forward, organised by the Flemish broadcasting network VRT, Peter Hinssen introduced us to a wonderful compound word, of the kind that is only possible in the German language: Eisenbahnscheinbewegung. It refers to the phenomenon whereby a traveller on a train that has stopped still thinks he is moving, because a moving train is passing in the opposite direction on the adjacent track. This part of the book challenges you to shatter that illusion.

The best defence against a Zoonotic is to be one.

1

START FROM YOUR CORE: YOUR UNFAIR ADVANTAGE

What constitutes an Unfair Advantage and how you can develop one is something that I described in detail in my previous book, *Unfair Advantage* (2019). Here I will confine myself to a summary of the most essential elements of the concept.

What is an Unfair Advantage?

Let me begin with a definition:

> 'An Unfair Advantage makes you extremely unique, very difficult to copy, and consistently distinctive, as a result of which you remain relevant and provide your customers with a magnetic added value over a long period. Everything you do and everything you bring to market is a consequence of this Unfair Advantage. Competitors envy your company, not the other way around. Your Unfair Advantage is always relative.'

In short, an Unfair Advantage is:
1. Extremely unique
2. Very difficult to copy
3. Consistently distinctive
4. Relevant
5. Relative

AN UNFAIR ADVANTAGE IS...

EXTREMELY UNIQUE	DIFFICULT TO COPY	CONSISTENTLY DISTINCTIVE	RELEVANT	RELATIVE
Your Unfair Advantage is unique and specific to your company and its product or service. It is authentic and an answer to the question: who am I, really? Your Unfair Advantage is part of your DNA. Perhaps you can already see it or perhaps it is only latently present.	Your Unfair Advantage is difficult or even impossible to copy. Others ask themselves 'How did they do that?' They are jealous, because they can't do what you do and make what you make. All they can do is buy it. Think, for example, of inside information, an unbeatable sales team or status as an authority.	Your Unfair Advantage differentiates you in a consistent manner from all other brands. This 'being different' is an asset and gives you an edge over your competitors, as well as often creating a surprise.	Your Unfair Advantage solves an existing central problem. Don't make the mistake of being unique in something that no one wants: the list of failed inventions is endless. Of course, your visionary insight might allow you to meet a latent need. But in that case, make sure you are a new Steve Jobs or Jeff 'Amazon' Bezos!	Your Unfair Advantage is sustainable, but will not last forever. Being unique is not the holy grail. Others will eventually overtake you. So what's next? How will you remain unique? Patents expire. Markets change. A Cheetah can never rest, never. They are always alert and on edge. Copycats and competitors are constantly snapping at your heels.

Source: *Unfair Advantage*

An Unfair Advantage allows you to play to your own strengths. You are so unique that in an ideal situation you would have no competitors. Surpassing you is almost impossible. Everybody envies you. Your 'being different' puts your rivals out of the game, even if they are bigger, faster and more powerful. Of course, the ideal of 'no competitors' is an illusion, but in your efforts to come as close as possible to this ideal you must constantly question all your actions, so that you can develop a flexible and unique business strategy that will maximise your chances of survival.

I know of many brands that think they are sufficiently unique. Sadly, they are nearly all 'me too' brands, which are 99.99 percent identical to their competitors. In this context, time and the competition are the key factors that determine whether you will get into difficulties or not. Unless, of course, you have a lead over your rivals – although nowadays such leads seldom last for long. Often, you will only survive because the competition decides to leave your market in peace. In other words, you operate in the inhibition zone of your competitors. It is only because others keep their distance or feel that the time is not yet ripe for a move that you can live. But this is a dangerous position to be in. If, after a time, a competitor decides to follow you across the inhibition zone or if you start to slow down, you will soon have a fatal collision. Before this happens, you need to find a new approach with more control. In short, it is high time to find an Unfair Advantage.

Three evolutions make necessary the development of an Unfair Advantage as a competitive strategy:

1. **MARKET**
   More market leaders with a quasi-monopoly rule the market.
2. **ACCESS**
   Anyone can do business and threaten your business.
3. **WORLD**
   Digital applications and artificial intelligence will increasingly reduce distances.

What are the seven advantages of a Cheetah?

I built the Unfair Advantage model around the seven advantages that make the Cheetah a successful hunter. Like the Zoonotic, the Cheetah is a metaphor that will help you, your team, your management and your stakeholders to focus on these advantages in daily practice and during strategic sessions. Each of the advantages displays a different strength, which will give you a competitive edge. It is in the interplay of these strengths that you will find the unique combination that will allow your company to shine.

1. **Speed**
   In the battle to win customers, the need for speed is essential. If you are faster than your competitors, you will beat them every time, even if their product or service is slightly better than yours. It is smarter to launch something that is 80 percent ready rather than to wait for 100 percent, only to then discover that someone else got to the market before you. Waiting is the worst word in the business world and will kill you if you wait too long. You can never be as ready as you ideally want to be. And you are seldom forgiven for slowness. People simply forget about you. The reverse side of the coin? The Cheetah is not a marathon runner and can only maintain its super-fast sprint for less than a minute. Short-term objectives are therefore the best strategy.

2. Focus

Cheetahs have black teardrops around their eyes. This is not only attractive, but also very useful. These markings help the Cheetah to focus. Did you know that a hunting Cheetah can spot its prey at a distance of five kilometres? This would not be possible without their black 'eye-shades', because the sun would blind them. A Cheetah never loses focus and can scan its surroundings for hours. In particular, this kind of focus is a strength of start-ups. They are almost obsessed by their objective and by the desire to make a difference. Once achieved, they move up a gear and focus on the next objective. Larger companies often lose focus, because they have to deal with so many different challenges. But this does not mean that focusing is impossible for large companies: when we launched the Yelo app at Telenet in 2010, it was an absolute priority, to which all other actions were subordinate. Focus helps you to find and reach your objectives.

3. Story

You never hear Cheetahs roar; instead, they purr. It is almost as if they tell stories, but stories in which they always remain readily identifiable, notwithstanding their discrete nature. Many young starters and disruptive companies understand this. They invest in a recognisable visual identity and in this way create the illusion that they are highly dangerous. But these stories must be authentic and should always emphasise your origins or what makes you different. Tip? Think, for example, about storytelling at the financial level. Tell stories about your vision and where you want to go with your company. People and the media will pick up what you say and spread it further.

4. Agility

In 2013, scientists concluded that, in addition to speed, the Cheetah's high success rate when hunting is due to its agility. Cheetahs are the Fred Astaires of the cat world. Their light and slender bodies allow them to manoeuvre, zig-zag, dive and turn with ease, even in the thick undergrowth of the savannah. Does your company also have this kind of agility? Can you change direction quickly? Can you respond to changing circumstances, whatever they are, without delay? The downside to agility is often a lack of consistency. Happily, the long and muscular tail of the Cheetah helps it to maintain direction and gives it balance during its sprint. Its paws are fitted with a kind of high-tech traction system. Agility must go hand in hand with strong leadership and a clear course of action.

5. Territory

Cheetahs live primarily in Africa and function best in dry and open savannah landscapes, liberally dotted with shrubs, termite mounds and clumps of grass that serve as observation posts. However, the Cheetah only remains strong as long as there is sufficient prey to let it thrive. If you want to grow, you have got to be where growth is to be found. Or in the words of Isabel Albers, editorial director at Mediafin and former editor-in-chief at *De Tijd* newspaper: a goldfish will only grow to the size that its bowl allows. Similarly, your company's environment – both its market and its location – will undoubtedly have an influence on its growth. In addition to the availability of growth channels, the size of the market will be a decisive factor in your results. The Cheetah's 'market', in the open plains of the savannah, is gigantic. But in today's digital business world you can also access the vast open plains of the international market with just a single click of a mouse. If you think it necessary, you can first test your Unfair Advantage in a smaller region before moving on to larger ones. And always remember that you need to take account of the local fauna and flora.

6. Resources

Cheetahs make use of existing resources. They do not construct their own nest, but build further on the things they find. My advice? Learn and copy from the best, but think carefully before you do so. Analyse what works for the other player and assess whether it can work for you. Do you need to change or improve something? Also remember to guard and protect your own resources. If you don't, your competitors will run away with them.

7. Network

Male Cheetahs live in groups and sometimes hunt together. Joining forces helps them to take on large prey. People also like to belong to small groups with a common purpose, as explained in the book *Tribe* by war journalist Sebastian Junger. Similarly, companies do not exist in isolation. In *The Network*

Always Wins Peter Hinssen explains why companies also need to work together in groups. The main reason? Because the world we live in is a network. Your network can help you with advice, financial capital and human capital. But care is also needed. Be on your guard against losing the things that make you different; otherwise, you will lose yourself – and your company!

Do the Unfair Advantage Cheetah test

The Unfair Advantage Cheetah test measures the Cheetah factors of your company. This will help you to understand the current situation and set priorities in your search for your Unfair Advantage.

1. The 49 strengths have a score from 49 to 1. The higher the score, the less easy a strength is to copy and the more future-proof it is. Look at the seven Cheetah advantages (speed, focus, etc …) in your company and link each of them to a maximum of three strengths. Write down the resulting score on the Cheetah scoreboard. This means that you will have a maximum of 21 strengths with a score. If you don't have a score for a particular advantage? In that case, your score is 0.

2. Calculate the score per strength and advantage, noting them down in the graphic (this will give you a bar chart). For extra visualisation, add the same scores in the rose (this will give you a spider diagram).

3. Add up the total score and follow the advice given.

Scores lower than 150: It is a miracle that your company is still alive. Even so, you are dead in the water. Perhaps you don't know it yet or are still in the denial phase, because this is a phase that can last for a long, long time. The slowness of your decline and death creates the illusion that everything is still okay. Some companies survive for decades with bad business practices, because they are fortunate that competitors leave them in peace. But when the competition finally decides to attack, you haven't got a chance. Before going any further, return to chapter 2 and carefully re-read the section that explains the advantages possessed by a Cheetah.

Scores between 150 and 450: You think competitively, but your actions are based on old and outdated models, with too little to make you seem decisively different. Use chapters 3 and 4 to make your company future-proof and to help you build an Unfair Advantage.

Scores between 450 and 550: You are competition-proof and clearly move with the times, but the final step is still missing. You need to ramp up your differentiation. Boost your strengths and eliminate (or at least improve) your weaknesses. Perhaps you are a young Cheetah and insight will come with more experience. Or perhaps you can add the finishing touch to your Cheetah status through a takeover or by working with others. Further perfect your Unfair Advantage using the methods outlined in chapters 5 and 6.

Scores higher than 550: You are already a player that others envy. You have reached the highest level of uniqueness and everyone looks up to your company. They all wonder how you have become so strong and what your next step will be. You collect gold medals like the Olympic wonder-swimmer, Michael Phelps. But never forget that the race is still on!

THE UNFAIR CHEETAH TEST?

HOW DOES YOUR COMPANY SCORE IN THE UNFAIR CHEETAH TEST?

In the Unfair Cheetah test we measure the Cheetah factor of your company. This will allow you to know your current position and show you which priorities to set in your search for your Unfair Advantage.

LET'S START ...

1. SPEED

49	Speed to Market	
48	Processes	
47	Work ethic	
46	Faster sales closing	
45	Short-term success	
44	Business principles	
43	Structural innovation	
TOTAL	**=**	

2. FOCUS

42	Vision	
41	Mergers and takeovers	
40	Niche	
39	Diversity	
38	Sustainability	
37	Price	
36	Business model	
TOTAL	**=**	

3. STORY

35	Culture	
34	Values	
33	Identity	
32	Recognisability	
31	Quality	
30	Design	
29	Imagedel	
TOTAL	**=**	

4. AGILITY

28	Innovation	
27	Lean innovation	
26	Cloud computing	
25	Entry barriers	
24	Passion	
23	Switching	
22	Tactics	
TOTAL	**=**	

5. TERRITORY

21	Speed to Market	
20	Processes	
19	Work ethic	
18	Faster sales closing	
17	Short-term success	
16	Business principles	
15	Structural innovation	
TOTAL	**=**	

6. RESOURCES

14	Artificial intelligence	
13	Intellectual property	
12	Information	
11	Knowledge	
10	Experience	
9	Technology	
8	Capital	
TOTAL	**=**	

7. NETWORK

7	Dream team	
6	Customers	
5	Micro-influencers	
4	Connections	
3	Partners	
2	Community	
1	Management	
TOTAL	**=**	
END TOTAL	**=**	

HOW BERNIE SANDERS BECAME A POP-UP ZOONOTIC

Bernie's Unfair Advantage is his rebellious nature, free from all hypocrisy and regard for etiquette. This finds expression in (among other things) his dress style. For example, for a highly formal event like the inauguration of a new president he chose to dress in a highly informal and unconventional way (an ordinary raincoat and excessively wide shoes).

It is precisely because of this mode of behaviour that Bernie has become a kind of pop-up Zoonotic in no time at all. Using social media and crowdfunding as a Superspreader, he has been able to raise several million dollars for good causes at exponential speed.

How do you find your Unfair Advantage?

This requires you to answer the following question: what makes your company extremely unique?

Once you have identified your Unfair Advantage, you can train yourself to use it in the best way,, so that you can maximise the benefits it can bring. We will find the answer to the above question by completing a series of seven exercises. These step-by-step exercises in funnel form will reveal everything you need to know to discover your Unfair Advantage.

The exercises will also prepare you to play the Unfair Business Game, by gradually getting you into the right kind of mindset. We will take a journey through the DNA of your company, but will also take a close look at what makes your customers tick. Your company only exists because these customers are willing to buy whatever it is you are selling. It is only thanks to your customers that you can survive, thrive and grow. The search for your Unfair Advantage goes hand in hand with customer obsession, which is the baseline of our company, Duval Union. If your Unfair Advantage does not respond to what your customers want or are waiting for, you will not only be Unfair but also unloved.

EXERCISE 1: WHAT IS YOUR LEADERSHIP DISCIPLINE?

In their book *The Discipline of Market Leaders*, Michael Treacy and Fred Wiersema divide market leaders into three categories:

1. Product leadership means that you conquer the market with a top product. The Canadian-American entrepreneur and Tesla boss Elon Musk understands perfectly that Tesla has product leadership in the field of electric cars and seeks to further exploit this position. Similarly, his Space X company, which specialises in space transportation, is also light years ahead of its rivals. Musk recently joked: 'I'd like to die on Mars. Just not on impact.' This clearly implies that the product is central and that his space craft will be of such high quality that a safe landing and return will be guaranteed. Another powerful example of product leadership is Apple, a company that continually strives to have the very best and/or most innovative product. What will be the next groundbreaking Apple device in the post-Steve Jobs era? Nobody knows, but there is every likelihood that it will take the market by storm.

2. Operational leadership means that your business processes are optimal. This way you can offer your customers streamlined, but high-quality products and offer stress-free services at an unbeatable price, with great ease of purchase. Ryanair and Colruyt are striking examples. Both are award-winners and give you smooth, acceptable service. They are cost leaders in monitoring their price structure, but often land on thin ice. The service can suffer from their cost-cutting approach. Remember the many cancelled Ryanair flights in 2017, which for many customers was a death blow. Ryanair fell below the limits for sufficient customer service. Watching over the basic quality of your products or services is a must. Note that the race for the lowest price never ends.

3. Customer partnership means that you place the customer at the heart of all you do. You think in terms of what the customer wants and focus constantly on his/her problems, challenges, objectives and experiences. Your contact with your customers is your strength and in most cases you build up an emotional relationship with them. Often, you do not have a standard product, but tend to specialise in customised items and services. The good thing about this method? There is less need to continually keep on convincing your customers; by and

large, they return automatically. Singapore Airlines, chosen in 2018 by TripAdvisor as the best airline in the world, is a good example of the virtues of a strong customer partnership. The pilots, air hostesses and all other members of the company's staff display a high degree of dedication, which guarantees a top-class flying experience.

If you want to become a market leader, Treacy and Wiersema say that you need to pick one of the three above-mentioned disciplines and then make sure that you achieve a 5-out-of-5 score in it. If you fail to go resolutely for one of these three options, you will often be making a strategic error or will end up with a combination of choices that are not wholly compatible in your case. If you do opt to mix two of the strategies, you need to score at least 3 out of 5 for both of them. If you don't, you will soon find yourself in serious difficulties.

EXERCISE 2: A DAY IN THE LIFE

Trying to imagine what your customers do in the course of an average day can be a real eye-opener. Perhaps it will make you realise just how little you really know about them. Maybe it will even make you ask when they are most likely to have time for you.

You need to see yourself as being a bit like an intruder in the lives of your customers. Like you, they are always busy. On top of that, they still need to find the time to work their way through the entire marketing funnel of your product or service. Focusing their attention, searching for information, considering their options, buying, installing and using: it all needs to be done. But if you know so little about your customers, how do you know the best moment and the best way to make your pitch to them? You don't? Then you had better book a return ticket to their world – before it is too late.

EXERCISE 3: WHO IS YOUR AVERAGE CUSTOMER?

In your search for your Unfair Advantage, it is only logical to ask yourself for whom you are providing your product or service. Even so, there are many entrepreneurs and marketeers who have no clear answer to this question: 'Our products and services are for everyone!', they claim. Newsflash: very few companies have products and services that are 'for everyone'. The exceptions tend to be fast-moving consumer goods with a low level of engagement, such as a jar of jam. I would recommend that all other companies think in terms of segmentation, which will help considerably when drawing up a marketing plan.

When making strategic choices, of which your search for your Unfair Advantage is the most important, it is useful to work with the concept of the 'average customer'. An average customer is the personification of a specific target group or an ideal customer. The characteristics and profile of this archetype will help you to set up, manage and develop the fundamentals of your company. In particular, it will simplify the translation of your strategy into the storytelling that you need to make your products or services attractive to your customer base. Ideally, it should be possible to describe an average customer in just a few brief terms. For example, an average Uber customer is a Millennial First-Digital Urban Worker.

EXERCISE 4: IDENTIFYING CUSTOMER TASKS, PAINS AND GAINS

Have you ever stopped to consider precisely what it is your customers wish to achieve? You can find out what you need to know using the Value Proposition Canvas. The first part of this practical and customer-oriented model is a description of the various tasks or jobs of your customers. This is then linked to areas of potential pain (problems) and gain (profit).

- The term 'customer tasks' covers everything that your customers wish to achieve, both professionally and privately, together with their related problems and needs. These tasks or jobs go much further than the purely functional. Emotional and status-driven tasks must also be included in the list. Emotional choices are often associated with finding safety or removing anxiety; status-driven choices are often motivated by a desire to belong. Let us consider, as an example, the customer tasks for Tesla customers. One of the functional tasks of an electric car is getting people safely from point A to point B. One of the possible status-driven tasks is the desire to be different or to make a good impression. The customers want to be seen with the car, since it creates an image of 'being successful'. In other words, the customers in the first instance have a need for 'transport' and opt to fulfil this need with 'driving an electric car'. The average Tesla customer does not seek 'driving a car without feeling guilty about the damage it causes to the planet'. Other average customers might seek this from other products and services, but the emotional task of Tesla for their average customer is the enhancement of their self-confidence and a feeling of safety.

- Pains are all the undesired consequences, problems, risks and obstacles associated with the tasks. Some negative effects are experienced by customers before, during or after the implementation of the tasks; others are more obstructive in nature. Thinking about such matters is always worthwhile, but happens far less frequently than you might think. In the Tesla example, the pain points are: flat battery, too few recharging points, more accidents or fines as a result of high speeds, a shortage of parking spaces, etc.

- Gains are all the benefits associated with the tasks, together with all the positive outcomes hoped for by your customers. Some gains are must-haves; others are wishes or expectations; yet others come as a surprise to the customers. With Tesla, the gains that complement the pains are: safe, stylish and powerful motoring, acceptable battery charging times, no problems with jealous drivers, compliments from your acquaintances, etc.

EXERCISE 5: DO YOUR PRODUCTS AND SERVICES MATCH PAINS AND GAINS?

It is now necessary to use the Value Proposition Canvas to see how far your offer corresponds with the pains and expected gains of your average customer. This allows you to check how far your products and services are able to generate pain relievers and gain creators, which will take away the problems of the customer, while at the same time also providing increased benefits.

- To see if you can generate pain relievers, ask yourself if your products and services save time, money and effort for the average customer; make him/her feel better; allow him/her to experience fewer problems, less anxiety, a greater sense of inclusion, etc. In short, do you remove the pains that are associated with the customer task(s)?

- To see if you can generate gain creators, ask yourself if your products and services make the life of your average customer easier; have positive social consequences; contribute towards his/her success or the realisation of his/her dreams; make him/her feel happier, etc. In short, do you satisfy (or preferably) exceed the average customer's gain expectations?

As a marketeer or company leader, you probably like to think in terms of functional pain relievers and gain creators. Your product managers will be able to tell you all about these things, so that summarising them is relatively simple. This is logical, because they are the people who are occupied day in and day out with refining the characteristics of your products and services. However, product characteristics are not necessarily the same thing as product valuation. In fact, they are two completely different things. An overlap between the two is not a default situation.

Be careful! People have a tendency to post-rationalise. If you ask someone why they buy something, the answer is often: 'Because I need that product', together with a whole series of other functional reasons. As a result, we think that people mainly make functional decisions. However, most purchases are charged with emotional or status-driven pain relievers and gain creators, either consciously or latently. So don't forget to focus on these aspects as well when carrying out this exercise.

EXERCISE 6: WHAT IS YOUR POSITION IN THE VALUE PYRAMID?

The pain relievers and gain creators in exercise 5 reveal the extent of the value that your products and services are able to give to the customer. You now need to check the relative importance of this value by positioning it on the value pyramid. Just like in a food chain, some links in the chain – and likewise some values – are more important than others. So just how important is your value? If you are at the top of a food chain, you are a hunter. If you are at the bottom of the chain, you are a prey. The value pecking order is as follows:

1. World-changing: you have a positive impact on society and the world.
2. Life-changing: you have a positive impact on people's lives.
3. Emotional: you give people a positive self-image.
4. Functional: you help people to meet practical needs and/or reduce risks.

Not every company seeks to appeal to a higher goal. Sometimes a product is just a product. However, every company can appeal to a higher goal if it wants to, and this is certainly what I would recommend. Having a purpose that goes beyond mere self-interest increases your company's or your brand's right to exist. The purpose or the 'why', as Simon Sinek has shown us, makes you stronger. If a bomb falls on your company, people will miss you. You are more than a company that simply wants money from its customers. You mean something. You have become irreplaceable. Why? Because you help people, perhaps change their lives and maybe even build a better world.

If you score low on the value pyramid, people will not care very much about your company. Your existence is likely to be transitory. Here today and gone tomorrow. Consider the fate of a company like Snap. Their social medium Snapchat was a strong product until Facebook boss Zuckerberg (after a failed takeover bid) decided simply to copy the function. Although young people in particular have remained faithful to Snapchat, its further growth was torpedoed. If you are looking for a storytelling functionality to meet the need of posting fleeting live images, you can just as easily use Facebook and Instagram.

If Snapchat had meant more than something purely functional – if, for example, it had been a platform that allows you to deal with uncertainties – it would have been more firmly rooted in people's hearts and its market share would have continued to grow. Unfortunately, however, this was not the case and Zuckerberg was able to snap up a significant portion of their market share. People were willing to tolerate Zuckerberg's 'copycat' tactics because Snapchat didn't mean enough to them.

Note that everything depends on authenticity. It is not to possible to climb your way rapidly up the value pyramid 'like a bolt from the blue'. An example? Consider Starbucks' 'Race Together' campaign, which was intended by CEO Howard Schultz to initiate conversations about racial problems over a cup of coffee. What did Schultz forget? He is a white millionaire who has never had any problems with racism. The campaign did indeed provoke considerable discussion, but not the kind Schultz had been hoping for. This shows that if your higher goal is too transparent, public opinion can soon turn against you. Or as a headline in

De Morgen once put it in relation to the exaggerations of the body-positivity trend: 'I don't need soap to tell me how I should feel!'

EXERCISE 7: WHAT MAKES YOUR COMPANY EXTREMELY UNIQUE?

To help you find out what makes your company extremely unique, I am pleased to introduce you to the concept of the Onliness Statement. It was at Duval Branding that I first discovered this concept for the differentiation of brands. In the search for your Unfair Advantage, it can also be used at the company level.

You can make your Onliness Statement by answering a series of simple questions: what, how, who, where, when and why? These basic questions will allow you to discover what makes your company unique and relevant.

> For motorbike manufacturer Harley-Davidson, the answers to these questions are as follows:
> - the only manufacturer of motorbikes;
> - that make big and noisy bikes;
> - for machos and wannabe machos;
> - primarily in the United States;
> - because they are part of a subculture;
> - in an age of decreasing personal freedom.
>
> The answers for the P&G multinational are:
> - the only producer of household articles;
> - with such a wide range of quality;
> - for parents (educators/carers);
> - worldwide;
> - who want to do everything possible to help their child succeed in life;
> - in an extremely competitive world.

You can see how the answers to the 'what' question begin with 'the only'. In these answers I have left out the Unfair Advantage element, simply confining myself to the category. But if you have an Unfair Advantage in your company, you already have a powerful answer to the 'what' question. Your Unfair Advantage is part of your company's DNA and is therefore automatically a part of your 'what'. This is the ultimate goal that you always need to keep in sight. In the Harley-Davidson example, this might be 'the only testosterone-driven manufacturer of motor-bikes'. And for P&G it might be 'a mother-transcendent company'. I emphasise the words 'might be': these are fictional answers that I have made up to illustrate my point as clearly as possible.

Three examples of an Unfair Advantage

An Unfair Advantage can often come from the most unexpected quarter. Here are three concrete examples:

Carrefour introduced a Wine Bot in one of their shops. The AI of this digital wine adviser helps customers to choose the best wines to go with their planned meals. This removes choice stress from the customers' shoulders and helps them to make better choices and/or discover new wines. The wine seller Vinetiq.eu from Puurs does something similar with its SOS Sommelier.

Just Russel offers a subscription system for the home delivery of dog food. This Belgian start-up makes use of a special algorithm to determine the most appropriate food mix for every kind of dog. At the same time, it also makes the purchasing process as easy as possible for the customers. Once again, choice stress is eliminated and the food for their four-legged friends is delivered promptly to their doorstep.

For the past two years, the digital communication company Marbles has been offering its employees an unlimited number of annual leave days. Recently, they have also made it possible for the employees to hire and fire people. Why is this an Unfair Advantage? Because it makes the employees super-motivated, which leads to better results, helps them to provide a better service to customers, and encourages them to learn new skills and to extend their networks.

INSIGHT

> ### How do you save a family business?

Because family businesses form the backbone of the Belgian economy, they probably have more reason than other larger companies to devote the necessary attention to the preservation of their Unfair Advantage. This was a point I discussed in the following conversation with Hans Hermans of *Trends* magazine.

'One of the main problems for family businesses is to differentiate themselves sufficiently. Once, they ruled the roost in their own region. If they were identical with another company in another region, so what? It made no difference. But today that is not the case. The digital transformation means that separate regions no longer exist. And when the regional boundaries disappeared, so too did the certainties of the past. To make matters worse, the corona crisis has sought out the weaknesses in every company and has driven many of them to the wall.

About 80 percent of companies are still doing reasonably well, but many of them are still using methods from the pre-internet era. The younger generations that have taken over family businesses in recent years are often all too aware of the danger this involves. They realise that they are perhaps only 36 months away from the end, unless they change from the way the company has been run in the past.

In the first decade of the new century, iTunes dominated its sector. But who still talks about iTunes? Spotify has wiped them off the map, because it offers a much more customer-oriented solution. They decide on your behalf what kind of music you like to hear. That is real service!

Belgian family businesses tend to make errors in three key areas. To begin with, they often don't know who their customers are, whereas that really needs to be your basis. How do your customers live? What occupies their thoughts? What are their objectives in life? You need to be obsessive but also very objective about your customers. If you aren't, you can be certain that there will be someone else who understands them better and serves them better.

Companies are sometimes so focused on their own part of the value chain that they fail to realise that others are continuing to change, getting bigger and better all the time. As a result, they sometimes find themselves unexpectedly cut out of the chain. A typical example is a supermarket that opens its own factory for meat processing. If you are a main meat supplier to this supermarket, you not only lose an important customer but also acquire a serious new competitor. This can be fatal.

You need to do whatever you can to eliminate links in the supply chain of which you are a part. For example, how can you make your own raw materials or how can you serve the end-users of your products directly? People find it hard to think exponentially. As a result, you often hear them say: 'Things won't change that quickly'. If the corona crisis has taught us anything, it is that some countries and their inhabitants stared at the approaching crisis like a rabbit staring immobilised into the headlights of an oncoming car. Corona is a classic example of an exponential epidemic, which is precisely why it was able to become a pandemic. In other words, we now know what exponential thinking is. It is up to our entrepreneurs to apply it in the future.

Just think of some of the things that we today regard as normal, but seemed unthinkable just a few years ago. People telephoning while riding a bike. Your weekly messages delivered to your front doorstep. So press the alarm bell whenever you hear someone say: 'That will never happen'. And react to pre-empt possible evolutions.

Yet even though the problems are life-threatening, I believe that every company has the ability to save itself within the 36-month timeframe. Perhaps for a few it is already too late, but most of them still have enough time and enough money to make the necessary structural changes.

What are the conditions for success? The willingness to adjust quickly and to make sacrifices. Some companies will need to give up some of their activities, so that they can develop in a more focused way, saving what is good and ditching the rest. Other family businesses that are already in a healthier position can immediately start searching for their Unfair Advantage and link this to their current activities.

Remember that technology is not the product that people are waiting for. We do not listen to Spotify because its technology is fantastic, but because its service is fantastic.

Spotify understands the user better than the user understands himself. It offers the ultimate in customer orientation, made possible by first-class technology. As does Uber and the wine advice offered by Carrefour or Vinetiq.eu. In each of these cases, it is the level of service that allows these companies to differentiate themselves from the rest. Having said that, other differentiating factors are also possible: you can have the cheapest products, like Colruyt, or the best product, like Tesla.

Imagine that your company can remove your customers' worries and provide them with a level of service that until recently was thought to be impossible. For example, that you can ensure that dog lovers always have a sufficient supply of exactly the right kind of food for man's best friend. Or that you can help food lovers to always have the right wine for all their favourite dishes. Would these customers be likely to choose your company in preference to one of your competitors? You bet they would!

Finding this kind of Unfair Advantage is one thing. Introducing it in practice is something else. Marketing is also about getting everyone inside the company to buy in to an idea. A marketeer who wants to be innovative needs to spend 80 percent of his energy internally on his colleagues and only 20 percent externally on his customers. You need to convince everybody that you are right. This is an aspect that is even more noticeable in the family businesses I have worked with. I don't simply tell them what they should do, but also need them to commit to the total package and be able to feel the resulting progress. Only then will the impact be permanent.'

Perhaps you have already found your Unfair Advantage and built on it successfully. Perhaps equally your competitors have now reacted to your advantage and found an answer to it. This results in a return to the status quo. However, the real danger can often come from a totally unexpected direction; from a sector that at first glance seems to pose little threat to your own. In the same way that the bird and the bat needed the pig before they could infect humans, so you too need to find a pig in another sector which, in combination with your existing Unfair Advantage, will allow you to create a new Zoonotic. At first, you will be able to stay under the radar. Your competitors will fail to see your different approach as something menacing, because it is so atypical. But as soon as your Superspreader is ready for action, you can start growing at an exponential speed. By the time this happens, it is already too late for your rivals to do anything about it, unless they had the foresight to prepare for the possible emergence of a Zoonotic. But were they really that smart? I doubt it.

(RED) BY BONO

The simplicity of the Red campaign by Bono is also its genius: patenting the colour red (spreader #1) as a means for a worldwide fundraising action (spreader #2) on behalf of AIDS research under the title (RED)(Zoonotic). It is also a classic example of the mindset of a Zoonotic leader. The campaign has not restricted itself to the direct sale of red-coloured INSPI(RED)T-shirts, but has also convinced iconic international brands to serve as influencers by launching a (RED) variant of their existing products onto the market. As a result, their customers can support a good cause without any extra effort, while at the same time treating themselves to – and differentiating themselves with – exclusive products. Thanks to the (RED) iPhone, the (RED) iWatch, the (RED) Durex, the (RED) Beats Solo 3 headphone, the (RED) Montblanc trolley cabin, the (RED) Vespa Prima Vera and many other similar luxury products, it has so far been possible to raise 650 million dollars for AIDS research (https://www.red.org/how-red-works).

HOW (RED) WORKS

(YOUR CHOICE.)

When you buy a (RED) product
or take part in a (RED) experience,
you help save lives.

(YOUR IMPACT.)

100% of the money contributed by
(RED) partners goes to the Global Fund to fight
two pandemics: AIDS and COVID-19.

SHOP (PRODUCT)^{RED}

ALL BRANDS ▾

BEATS SOLO3 WIRELESS HEADPHONES
$299.95

APPLE IPHONE 12 (PRODUCT)RED
From $799.00

DUREX CONDOM EXTRA SENSITIVE, 42 COUNT
$14.99

THERABODY THERAGUN ELITE
$399.00

UBUNTU LIFE MASK DESIGNED BY BARO SARRE
$15.00

(RED) ORIGINALS INSPI(RED) T-SHIRT
$30.00

RONALD DRAPER ENDU(RED) PIN
$19.85

MONTBLANC #MY4810 TROLLEY CABIN
$965.00

Source: https://www.red.org/products

The (RED) case illustrates perfectly what I call the mindset of a Zoonotic leader. But that is not always how it happens. By way of contrast, consider the KDACHTETNI project. I have huge respect for the action launched by Yamina Krossa, who via the sale of T-shirts and sweaters, in collaboration with Kleir, raises money to support the fundamental cancer research carried out at the Free University of Brussels by Professor Dr Damya Laoui. But how much more impact might this extremely worthwhile project have had if, right from the very beginning, it had set its sights beyond our national borders and had sought an international clothing brand (or at the very least a European one) as its partner? KDACHTETNI is a cute play on words, but (regrettably) one that only works in Flanders, whereas breast cancer and the need for research are not confined to our region. Be that as it may, please do not let these critical thoughts of mine prevent you from supporting this wonderful initiative: https://destination400.vubfoundation.be

1. What is the creative idea and who benefits from it?

The (RED) project is an idea developed by Bono and Bobby Shriver, which was launched at the World Economic Forum in 2006 with the intention of using the marketing power of the private sector to raise funds for the AIDS campaign in Africa. It began with a simple sketch on a serviette, but it evolved into a unique and powerful collaboration between leading international brands. The project had three objectives:

- To make it easier for consumers to donate money to good causes.
- To give the partner companies a profitable way to support a meaningful and worthwhile objective.
- To provide a sustainable source of income for the Global Fund to Fight Against AIDS.

(RED) has given the synergy between marketing and fundraising a new dynamic. It is the world's largest consumer-supported fundraising activity for a humanitarian purpose.

2. What makes it possible for the idea to be shared? What are the memorable buzzwords or hashtags?

The brilliant thing about this campaign is its simplicity. Its most memorable aspect is its emphasis on the colour red, the colour of blood. Historically, it calls up associations of courage and sacrifice. In Europe, red symbolises passion. In Asia, it is equated with happiness and prosperity. Thanks to Bono and Africa, red now also exemplifies how companies can work together to achieve something worthwhile other than profit.

3. How can you use time pressure to accelerate the speed of development?

The campaign combines altruism and consumerism. In the first year, 22 million dollars were raised. According to research carried out by Cone Inc. from Boston, 89 percent of Americans between the ages of 13 and 25 years are prepared to change to brands that support good causes, providing the product prices are comparable. The rapid progress of the disease in Africa added significant time pressure to the situation: in 2005 alone, 1,200 children were born with AIDS each day.

UNDER THE
MICROSCOPE

4. How do you get the support of big names and how do you find a match with important influencers?

It goes without saying that in this instance the international fame of Bono, who has been described as one of the World's Greatest Leaders, was the crucial factor for success.

5. How can you use a memorable and compact video?

In the 1980s and the 1990s, AIDS was a worldwide infection that received widespread coverage in the media, often with harrowing images that stuck in the mind. Similarly, the film *Philadelphia*, with Tom Hanks in the leading role and music by Bruce Springsteen, touched a chord with the wider public, as did the death of rock icon Freddy Mercury.

6. How does this campaign motivate and demonstrate both engagement and altruism?

Every generation is known for one specific reason or another. We, the (RED) generation, want to be the generation that defeated AIDS. This demands collaboration between consumers and companies, who are prepared to donate part of their profits to this noble cause.

7. How can you ensure that the threshold to participate is kept as low as possible?

Thanks to (RED), doing good has never been so easy or so much fun, both for customers and for the partner companies. For example, American Express saw its brand familiarity significantly increase among younger people, whereas at GAP the project had a positive impact on the engagement of staff and improved the profile of people applying for a job with the company. At the same time, the INSPI(RED) T-shirt became the bestselling article in their range. Some of the partners even go as far as to have their products made or at least packaged in Africa, which provides much needed additional employment for the local population.

2

A ZOONOTIC LEADER GIVES THE KICK-OFF

Perhaps your company does not immediately have the necessary financial resources to neutralise a Zoonotic that moves into your sector. If this is the case, you urgently need to develop a Zoonotic strategy of your own, because there is a very good chance that in the years ahead the impact of hostile Zoonotics will increase significantly. Zoonotic leadership therefore requires you to trigger a viral strategy in your own company. But you can't do it alone. Help from a like-minded team is essential.

Just because your company already has a strong focus on digitalisation, this does not mean that you are a disruptive force. To create and develop a Zoonotic strategy, you need a Zoonotic leader who – to put it mildly – has an unusual way of doing things, a style that may frighten or even repel many people. Even so, if you want your company to be ready to meet the challenges of the future in the long term, you need to start preparing NOW to turn yourself into a Zoonotic. Look for, find or become your own Elon Musk. Switching to a Zoonotic style of leadership has important positive consequences. So don't wait any longer.

How can you recognise a Zoonotic leader?

108

HOW DO YOU BECOME A ZOONOTIC?

1. **Cheetah:** The Zoonotic leader has the extreme reaction speed and sharp focus of a Cheetah.
2. **Unfair**: The Zoonotic leader is fanatical about exploiting the importance of an Unfair Advantage as a starting point and is willing to explore new and latent needs.
3. **No Status Quo**: The Zoonotic leader has no interest in the status quo. He/she thinks about what might be possible and not simply about what is practicable. A Zoonotic leader thinks and acts counter-cyclically. He/she goes against the current trends in the economy.
4. **Resilience**: The Zoonotic leader has the necessary drive and determination to bounce back time after time when things do not go as planned. His/her motto is: Try, Fail, Learn, Repeat.
5. **Network**: The Zoonotic leader understands networks and invests in them heavily, because he/she knows, as Peter Hinssen rightly says, that 'the network always wins'. Or in the words of Stanley McCrystal: 'It takes a network to defeat a network.'
6. **Creative**: The Zoonotic leader is a creative hacker who always keeps his field of vision wide open, constantly searching for new opportunities both inside and outside the company's current market.
7. **The Moonshot**: The Zoonotic leader seeks out like-minded partners, both inside and outside his/her own company, with the aim of moving beyond the limitations of 'quarterly thinking'. He/she embraces the unexpected and prepares the company culture to deal with it.
8. **Team talent**: The Zoonotic leader has the talent to attract the right team members to the company and the necessary empathy to inspire them.
9. **Ethical**: The Zoonotic leader believes in Stakeholder Capitalism and not exclusively in Shareholder Capitalism or State Capitalism. Failing to respect this ethical vision increases the likelihood that your company will turn into a Predatory Zoonotic.

Whether you find the Zoonotic leader inside or outside your own company or whether you have the guts to become a Zoonotic leader yourself, the aim must always be 'to boldly go where no one has gone before'.

A Zoonotic leader must be 200 percent dedicated to his/her task. This is something that Jack Dorsey, the CEO of Twitter, seemingly failed to appreciate. When this happens, the financial analysts are severely critical: 'With a part-time CEO you get part-time revenue growth.' This was a reference to the fact that revenue at Twitter was growing much more slowly than their number of users, whereas other social media platforms were successfully able to increase revenue growth faster than user growth.

One way to get a good sense of what it takes to become a Zoonotic leader is by studying a few concrete examples. These will be spread throughout this chapter. Here is the first one.

ROLE MODEL>
JACINDA ARDERN: ZOONOTIC
LEADERSHIP DOWN UNDER

Why was Jacinda Ardern re-elected as Prime Minister of New Zealand with a landslide victory? According to the news website of the Flemish broadcaster VRT, the reason was not hard to find: 'The victory of the 40-year-old Ardern, premier since 2017, was Labour's best result in the last 50 years. "These are no ordinary times and this was no ordinary election," said Ardern during her victory speech, referring to the fact that the declaration of the results had been delayed by a month because of the corona crisis. "There was great uncertainty and anxiety, and we were able to convince people that we were the antidote."'

Her success in dealing with the corona crisis is one of the main explanations for her election victory. As we did in Europe, the New Zealanders went into lockdown in March 2020. However, the number of infections and fatalities remained limited, and in June the premier was able to declare that the last patient had been cured. 'I did a little dance of joy,' she said at the time. The New Zealanders thought that they were rid of corona, but celebrated too soon. In August, a new outbreak occurred in Auckland, the largest city in the country, which led to a new set of stringent restrictions and the delay of the national election.

Ardern's prompt and resolute approach, with clear and, above all, empathic communication, gained her much praise.

For example, at the start of the lockdown she held a question-and-answer session for members of the public from her bedroom. Her constant reference to 'The team of 5 million' (the total number of people living in New Zealand) caught on throughout the nation, as did her slogan 'Be kind, be strong'. It is a brilliant example of the unifying use of language.

What exactly did her resolute approach involve? New Zealand immediately closed its borders and introduced a quick and effective system of contact tracing, controlled quarantine and extensive testing. Of course, it was easier for an island nation in the middle of the Pacific Ocean to control its borders than it was for many other countries. Even so, there were still some initial problems that needed to be dealt with. For example, there were still instances where foreign travellers returning to New Zealand brought COVID back into the country. At a different level, some of the media also accused Ardern of a lack of transparency.

Ardern was helped by the fact that corona was not the first crisis that she and the New Zealand people had been forced to confront in recent times. In March 2019, more than 50 people were killed in a terrorist attack on two mosques in the city of Christchurch, carried out by a right-wing extremist from Australia. In the aftermath of this terrible tragedy, the prime minster was widely praised for her warm and human approach. She went immediately to the stricken city to talk with survivors and next of kin, offering them and all New Zealanders a message of solidarity and hope. She backed this up by quickly introducing new and much tighter gun-control legislation. Later that same year, in December, she displayed similar qualities of empathy combined with action when a sudden volcanic eruption on White Island cost 21 people their lives.

Courage, speed, a broad vision and an authentic and empathic communication style. These a just a few of the important characteristics of a Zoonotic leadership style.

A Zoonotic leader is a creative hacker

Jürgen Ingels is an entrepreneur and investor who made his fortune with Clear-2Pay, a platform that simplified payments made between different banks. He was once a guest in my Reading Room, where he emphasised the importance of creativity and hacking as two of the most essential qualities that a future-oriented leader must possess. With 'hacking', he does not mean the illegal capture and manipulation of other people's software, but rather a creative process that companies nowadays can employ more than ever to make themselves more efficient. This involves making use of short-cuts that others have not yet seen, an approach that actually corresponds with the original meaning of 'hacking', which meant the solving of problems in an original manner by creative minds who were able to see beyond the existing rules. Needless to say, in our modern world technology also plays a crucial role in this process. Ingels believes that there is a need for more companies to work in parallel, so that they do not confine their field of vision to just a single sector, but are open to opportunities that may arise in various sectors that can provide them with new and decisive short-cuts. This, of course, is precisely the essence of a business Zoonotic: combining ideas from two different sectors to create something totally new. What's more, this is largely a creative process, in which your own ingenuity allows you to see how an approach in one sector can provide a solution for a problem in a completely different sector.

A good example is the dilemma currently experienced by many people who want to find the right balance between diet and health. According to Ingels, a scanner in your kitchen could help you to know precisely what ingredients you have in your fridge and how they can best be combined and portioned for someone in your specific situation. Sounds futuristic? Ingels takes his thinking much further than that! He already envisages the use of a robot that can be installed in your body via nanotechnology, whose task is to constantly monitor a number of crucial parameters in your blood and transmit them to an application that will then indicate which nutrients you need and therefore which diet you should follow at that particular time. In short, made-to-measure dietary advice appropriate for your current medical condition. For people affected by certain illnesses or diseases, this could help them to avoid a serious worsening of their situation. But Ingels also expects that in future the wider population will also pay increasing attention to the importance of healthy food. Consequently, to complete his out-of-the-box thinking, he contemplates the development of a further nanorobot that will auto-matically order all the food and drink you need.

According to Ingels, this means that the education system, in addition to foster-ing knowledge and skills, will also need to focus more on developing the creativi-ty of our young people, teaching them how to make connections between matters that at first glance seem to have nothing to do with each other. To support his argument, he offers this anecdotal example from his own family. When his son asked for a new and more powerful computer that would allow him to play new and more powerful games, Ingels was initially reluctant to agree. He thought it was 'too easy' as a solution. Consequently, he arrived home a few days later with a new computer in a box – but it was all in pieces! If his son wanted a new computer, he would first have to learn how to put it together. And, after hours of searching on the internet for guidance and with a little help from his friends, he succeeded. As a result, he now had his new computer, but he also had a better knowledge of and interest in hardware and software.

Ingels follows up this interesting story with an important piece of advice for par-ents: don't focus too much on the subjects for which your children only score 5 out of 10; encourage them instead to improve still further in the subjects at which they already excel and stimulate them to work together with others to learn more about the subjects that are clearly not their strengths.

In the companies with which he is associated, Jürgen Ingels is always on the look-out for a hack that can result in a time reduction. His key question is this: how can we save time through the simplification of our processes? Because nowadays time is more important than ever. Successful companies are the companies that think quick and act quick to beat their competitors to the marketplace.

ROLE MODEL>
WIBE WAGEMANS: A DUTCH PIONEER AND SERIAL ENTREPRENEUR IN THE VALLEY

Wibe Wagemans is a Dutch tech entrepreneur, who was the first to develop an AI-bot and a mobile online video game. He made important contributions to the success (amongst others) of Angry Birds, Big Fish, and Huuuge. He has won the Cannes Golden Lion Award and holds the world record for No. 1 hits in the App Store. He worked for Gillette and Nokia, before setting off to find fame and fortune in Silicon Valley. Together with journalist Eva Schram, who has also lived and worked for years in the Valley, he wrote the book *The Secret of Silicon Valley*. This book is interesting, not only for ambitious entrepreneurs who are considering a move to the US, but also for those who want to know how their competitors in the Valley build up their companies. It is full of useful lessons that will allow you to innovate more effectively and to deal strategically with access to capital, markets and talent, as well as telling you the best way to lead and organise governance in your company. The book emphasises that today's entrepreneurs need to realise that the familiar patterns of the past are on the way out – for good.

'The world seems to be an even crazier place, if you realise that today, apart from a few exceptions:
- Automobile innovation comes from Germany.
- AI-innovation comes from Boston.
- Mobile innovation comes from Finland.
- Film industry innovation comes from Hollywood.
- Electronic innovation comes from Japan.
- Energy innovation comes from Houston.
- Cloud innovation comes from London.
- Financial innovation comes from New York.
- Software innovation comes from India.'

A Zoonotic leader is performance-driven

In *The Secret of Silicon Valley* Frank Slootman, the CEO of data-warehouse company Snowflake, says that the leader in an innovative tech company must be highly performance-driven, as well as needing to emphasise three key matters:

1. **Speed:** 'If I hear that I am only going to get something next week, I say: "How about tomorrow morning?" People work at a slower pace than they are capable of. A leader needs to increase the tempo. Every meeting, every conversation is an opportunity to move up a gear or two. If you keep on doing this, eventually you create a culture where people regard working at top speed as standard. If the speed of a company accelerates, that changes everything. It's like a kind of magic. Everything goes faster and easier.'

2. **Focus:** 'No distractions, no other objectives. All that matters is our core business mission. We are not interested in anything else. Intensity is one of the most important management concepts. People often think that they are focused, but don't really know what focus involves. To be truly focused, you need to give up a lot. I frequently attend the board meetings of other companies and it might happen that the CEO gives a run-down of a list of ten priorities. If you've got that many priorities, you might as well have none at all. That's not focus. I always ask: "What is the one thing? What is the most important thing of all?"'

3. **Higher standards:** 'People have the tendency to make compromises on quality, perhaps because something takes a lot of energy. I keep on telling them that it is precisely this energy that they need to invest to make sure of taking things to a higher level. The business world is full of people who tolerate average quality. But if you tell people that something is not good enough, you unexpectedly start getting better results.'

In my book *Unfair Advantage* I wrote that speed and focus are the two most important qualities of a Cheetah, an animal that seems to have been born for perfection.

ROLE MODEL>
CONSTANTIJN OF ORANGE-NASSAU
RANGE: TECH PROMOTER WITH ROYAL BLOOD

Constantijn of Orange-Nassau is a special envoy for Techleap, a state-financed organisation to promote Dutch start-ups and scale-ups. By working with Techleap, his aim is to make The Netherlands the best technology scale-up and start-up ecosystem in Europe.

Techleap.nl not only brings together tech-entrepreneurs in the hope that they will be able to inspire each other, but also supports them via network contacts in their search for capital or the development of an international strategy, as well as helping to turn academic expertise into concrete products and services.

Techleap.nl is not really a start-up accelerator like Y Combinator in the US, but they do have a programme to assist start-ups that want to join Y Combinator in order to increase their chances of success. This involves them asking entrepreneurs who have already made the switch to Y Combinator to share their experiences, so that other Dutch founders will have a better idea of what to expect.

Y Combinator is unique and has no equivalent in The Netherlands. That the prince takes his role with Techleap seriously became evident when he actually threatened to resign his position as an ambassador if the Dutch cabinet failed to show more ambition. And it worked! Less than six months later, the Ministry of Economic Affairs announced that it was pumping 65 million euros into start-ups and scale-ups, although not without some serious discussions and a number of pointed text messages between the prince and Prime Minister Rutten. Of this 65 million, 50 million will now go to Techleap.nl, the organisation for which the prince is clearly a highly effective standard bearer.

IQ is important, but so is EQ

Travis Kalanick, Steve Jobs and Elon Musk are undoubtedly inspirational leaders, but leaders of this kind are often also authoritarian, with a low level of EQ. That now seems set to change. EQ is becoming increasingly important as a key leadership quality. In today's world, emotional intelligence is necessary to better understand your customers, so that you can make better products for them and avoid turning into a Predator Zoonotic. At the same time, a high EQ also makes you a better colleague or boss.

I follow Schram and Wagemans when they say: 'Self-awareness is fundamental. It means that you understand your own emotional condition and know the things that motivate and mobilise you. But it also means that you are acutely aware of your own shortcomings. How afraid are you of these shortcomings and are you able to allow others to make them good? The greatest skill in emotional intelligence is learning to listen with an emotional antenna.

If you listen with an emotional antenna, you implicitly give your agreement that people can tell you the things that you need to hear, even if it is not always pleasant. Instead of building a wall around yourself, you are accessible. In both a physical and an emotional sense. As already mentioned, this takes self-awareness. But it also takes self-confidence: you know who you are and what you can do. This is closely related to being open for feedback, but goes much further. Having an emotional antenna allows you to correct your own error or bad habit before someone else points it out, because you see yourself as an indivisible part of a whole.'

Jan De Schepper, co-author of *ConneXion: 7 Paradoxes for the Modern Leader* was another of the guests in my online Reading Room. For their book, the authors asked numerous business leaders whether or not they thought of themselves as a good coach. Around 80 percent answered positively. But when their colleagues and personnel were asked whether or not their boss was an empathic leader, only 15 percent answered in the affirmative. This immediately exposes the crux of the leadership problem. To be a good leader, you need to pass this kind of reality check with flying colours.

Inge Van Belle

Herculean Alliance

Klaus Lommatzsch

Duval Union

'In our recent book *Employee engagement, what else? Tried and tested marketing insights for a better HR policy*, I (together with Klaus Lommatzsch) described the three key components that are necessary to be able to operate as a team and to create trust: security, vulnerability and purposefulness. Of course, it helps enormously if the leader is able to create these conditions. In this context, security and vulnerability are particularly important.

Security

If you are recruited as a new employee in a company, it is important that you feel safe as quickly as possible within your group of new colleagues. This may sound self-evident, but it often runs contrary to how human beings think, feel and act. Most of us are suspicious of people who we do not know and it can sometimes take a long while before we feel we can trust them. Our brains are programmed to be wary of strangers, to be on the alert for danger signals, and to conform to the wishes of our hierarchical superiors. These are all characteristics that in the distant past could make the difference between life and death for our ancestors, struggling to survive on the savannah. In *The Culture Code*, Daniel Coyle contends that the first condition for giving trust is that you feel safe within a group. For this reason, it is a key task for any team to make it possible for everyone, and especially newcomers, to be themselves and to express their feelings. Team members must also know that they are allowed to make mistakes. It is only when these conditions have been met that a person will be able to feel safe within a team. Safe teams can be distinguished from others by the greater number of signals of togetherness they transmit: more interactions, short conversations, jokes, gestures of physical contact, etc.

Vulnerability

Making yourself vulnerable might sound a bit odd in a business context, but it is just as crucial as creating a feeling of security. If you make a mistake, can you talk about it with others and search together to find a solution? It is only by admitting your mistakes and discussing them that you will be able to learn from them and avoid repeating them in the future. In this respect, the leader must set a good example by also having the courage to make himself/herself vulnerable, so that others will not be afraid to do the same.

When I asked my own team whether or not I am an empathic leader, they immediately gave me a number of concrete examples to suggest that I was. Okay, examples are not exact figures, but it was still a positive indication and a positive experience. My business partner Frederic Vanderheyde and I both attach huge importance to the human factor in our business culture. Even in Cheetah teams it is necessary to have moments of calm and consultation. In this respect, Paul Van Den Bosch sees a parallel with top sport, where such moments are known as super-compensation.

Super-compensation means that you need a brief period of rest, so that you can build up your strength and gain even more speed. You need to give your muscles a chance to recover, so that you can come back stronger and faster than ever before. Jan De Schepper compares this with the human brain. Your brain is just like a single giant muscle, which occasionally needs to have some rest if you want it to perform better in future. 'Business is not a marathon, but a series of short sprints with periods of rest in between.'

The way you give feedback to your team members is 'the proof of the pudding' of your empathic leadership. This is doubly important in periods and situations of uncertainty, such as the corona crisis. For me, this period sometimes felt like suffering a defeat at sport. I was like the supporter of a football team that had been beaten by an invisible opponent. And, like a fanatical fan, I was forced to wait impatiently on the sidelines until the next match could be played. My dominant emotion was powerlessness, but I didn't lose heart. No, because my team and I are not Calimeros; we are Cheetahs! For this reason, we decided to share our expertise free of charge with our network and in eight months no fewer than 6,000 people were offered our free content via LinkedIn. When the lockdown was announced, we were momentarily downhearted, but we soon bounced back. If you are in business, you cannot afford to let powerlessness overcome you. Remember that setbacks are only temporary, emphasises Jan De Schepper.

According to De Schepper, it was only to be expected that corona would have an impact on all of us and on our leadership style. But business is an activity that never stops; it just keeps on going. 'A football match stops after 90 minutes, but a company doesn't. In a company, the flow continues.' As a result, the feeling of defeat seldom lasts for long. To assist this 'recovery process', De Schepper lists five important things that you need to take into account as a leader in time of crisis:

1. Remain very positive and enthusiastic at all times.
2. Maintain good contact with the people around you.
3. Adjust your objectives at every level.
4. Focus less on results and more on connections.
5. Remind your people every day of your vision for the future.

ROLE MODEL >
ANGELA MERKEL: A LEADER WITH
A EUROPEAN VISION

When Angela Merkel announced in 2019 that she would not be a candidate for a further mandate as chancellor of Germany, many observers thought that she would be a 'lame duck' until the new elections in September 2021. However, that was before the corona pandemic struck. The crisis gave her a further opportunity to prove herself as a reliable and determined leader. In part because of her scientific background as a physicist, she was able to understand the dangerous power of a viral pandemic better than any other political leader.

At the moment of writing, Germany is one of the most successful countries at dealing with the pandemic and polls show that Merkel enjoys the confidence of 83 percent of the population. Her party, the CDU, can count on the support of 40 percent of German voters. These are figures that would have been unthinkable at the start of 2020. But Merkel was not content to focus exclusively on Germany; she was also concerned about tackling the crisis at a European level. In this respect, it was a stroke of good fortune that in 2020 it was Germany's turn to assume the presidency of the European Council. But the fact that her country also invested much more than it will ever see back in the 500 billion euro European emergency fund, which she set up with the French President Macron, proves beyond doubt that she had the vision to think as an international – rather than a national – leader .

Her strengths are her sharp analytical mind, her pragmatic
approach and her empathic style of communication

A Zoonotic leader promotes Stakeholder Capitalism and Good Karma AI

I am strongly attracted by the Stakeholder Capitalism Manifesto of Klaus Schwab, founder of the World Economic Forum in Davos. Although his associated book has not yet been published at the moment of writing, the press have given clear details about the basic principles.

Schwab makes a distinction between three economic models. The first is Shareholder Capitalism, the model that is most commonly applied by Western companies. The ultimate aim of this model is the maximisation of profit for the shareholders. The second model is State Capitalism, where the government determines the direction of the economy, as is the case, say, in China. For example, when the Ant Group, with its easy-to-pay, borrow and invest app, threatened the payment system controlled by the Chinese state, the authorities quickly stepped in to neutralise the threat. Jack Ma, the co-founder of the e-commerce giant Alibaba and the majority shareholder in the Ant Group, was summoned to Peking for a reprimand and to make clear precisely who runs the Chinese economy. The third model is Schwab's Stakeholder Capitalism. In this model, private companies are seen as 'trustees of society', whose benefits they must serve.

Although in recent decades Shareholder Capitalism and State Capitalism have both improved the living standards for tens of millions of people, Schwab argues that Stakeholder Capitalism is better suited to deal with the major societal and climatological challenges of the world today. He actually first launched this concept as long ago as 1971, when the first World Economic Forum was held. This Davos Manifesto emphasised the responsibility of companies towards all their stakeholders. With the founding the World Economic Forum, it was his intention to help politicians and businessmen (and women) to make this possible.

The reason why more and more people and more and more companies are now starting to take this message seriously is the 'Greta Thunberg' effect. This youthful Swedish climate activist has shown the world that the current economic system is placing an intolerable burden on our planet and risks jeopardising the future of our young people. If you add to this the fact that the Millennials and Generation Z no longer wish to work for or buy from companies that focus exclusively on profit for their shareholders, the result is a cocktail of discontent that will make any sensible company think carefully about its approach. A growing number of companies are realising that their future is increasingly dependent not only on the well-being of their customers, but also on the well-being of their personnel and of society as a whole.

In his column for *De Tijd*, Peter De Keyzer pointed out that we need to be careful not to throw away the baby with the bathwater. Companies are the motor of our prosperity. They must therefore be able to demonstrate that they are part of the solution for the problems of Shareholder Capitalism. 'A company that thinks about its own future must show that it is at least as concerned about the future of the planet and of mankind. It can do this by planning and implementing concrete measures that benefit the climate, the environment and society at large. Vague promises, distant ambitions and transferring the responsibility to government will no longer be good enough. Companies that do not show that they are part of the solution will henceforth be considered as part of the problem. Today's politicians, activists, stakeholders and citizens will be satisfied with nothing less. (...) Companies are our best allies for dealing with the climate problem. Through its daily contact with its customers, personnel and suppliers, a company is closer to the public and has a better understanding of their concerns than the politicians. Moreover, major companies also have more influence and impact than politicians. They can reach millions or even billions of people worldwide and can take and implement decisions faster than any government in the world.'

An environmental defence group drags Shell in front of a court

A concrete and current example of Stakeholder Capitalism in action is the court case that seven NGOs and 19,000 ordinary citizens have initiated in The Netherlands against Royal Dutch Shell, one of jewels in the crown of the Dutch business world. The petitioners are demanding that RDS cuts its CO_2 emissions by half by 2030, since they argue that an effective environment policy in The Netherlands is not possible without the active collaboration of Shell, which emits twice as much CO_2 as the rest of the Dutch economy in total. They claim that this represents an infringement of the human rights of all Dutch citizens. At the time of writing, no final judgement has yet been made, but the Belgian professor Bart Kerremans thinks that the plaintiffs have little chance of success, because they have based their case on the Paris Climate Agreement, which is an agreement between nations and not between companies. Shell is only legally bound by the terms of the environmental permit drawn up and issued by the Dutch government. Having said that, there has already been another similar case where the Dutch government was instructed by a civil court to strengthen its environmental norms. So who knows?

Leaving aside the judicial arguments about the extent to which this kind of case represents a breach of the fundamental separation of powers, it is nevertheless a clear signal that in future stakeholders will demand to play a more active role. What is currently a series of seemingly isolated cases may in time grow to become a global Zoonotic. To avoid this possibility, it is in the companies' own interests not to ignore these signals and to embrace Stakeholder Capitalism instead. Don't forget that the notorious Dieselgate scandal also began innocently enough with a single complaint by a relatively small NGO in the United States, only later to be blown up to Zoonotic proportions that brought the entire automobile sector into disrepute.

In the updated version of the Davos Manifesto a number of ethical principles have been emphasised, such as the wish that companies should pay their 'fair share of taxes'; that there must be zero tolerance for corruption; respect for human rights throughout the supply chain; and the creation of a level playing field for the so-called 'platform economy'.

This will require the development of new metrics, for which the Sustainable Development Goals (SDGs) of the United Nations can serve as a roadmap. These metrics cover four key domains.

THE FOUR PILLARS

PRINCIPLES OF GOVERNANCE	PLANET	PEOPLE	PROSPERITY
The definition of governance is evolving as organizations are increasingly expected to define and embed their purpose at the centre of their business. But the principles of agency, accountability and stewardship continue to be vital for truly 'good governance'.	An ambition to protect the planet from degradation, including through sustainable consumption and production, sustainably managing its natural resources and taking urgent action on climate change, so that it can support the needs of the present and future generations.	An ambition to end poverty and hunger, in all their forms and dimensions, and to ensure that all human beings can fulfil their potential in dignity and equality and in a healthy environment.	An ambition to ensure that all human beings can enjoy prosperous and fulfilling lives and that economic, social and technological progress occurs in harmony with nature.

Source: World Economic Forum

Getting started with the Value Pyramid

In order to make people better aware of the SDG objectives, during my workshops I make use of a set of cards, as depicted in the Value Pyramid below. However, I do not arrange the cards in pyramid form, but leave them in a random order. I ask the participants to pick out the five cards they think are the most important and arrange them in order of priority, with the most important card at the top of the resultant pyramid. In this way, I challenge them to think about the extent to which their company effectively pursues a broad-based higher purpose.

A self-transcending purpose – a purpose that goes beyond your own mere self-interest – gives a company a greater legitimacy. The purpose or 'the Why', as Simon Sinek tells us, makes you stronger. It means that people will miss you if you are no longer there. You are more than a company that simply wants to extract as much money as possible from its customers. You have become unmissable. You signify something. Why? Because you help people and perhaps even change their lives. Who knows, you might even make the world a better place.

According to the *Davos Manifesto*, the criteria for shared value creation must, in addition to the classic financial criteria, now also include 'environmental, social, and governance' (ESG) criteria. It seems that the 'Big Four' accounting companies are already working along these lines. Another aspect that needs to be addressed is the remuneration awarded to managers, the levels of which must also take greater account of the above-mentioned new metrics for long-term shared value creation.

Last but not least, companies must also realise that they, too, are important stakeholders in the future. It goes without saying that companies must continue to focus on their core competencies and their entrepreneurial mindset, but they must also work together with other stakeholders to improve the world in which they operate. In fact, that must be their supreme objective.

WORLD-CHANGING

World-Changing

LIFE-CHANGING

Equality

Self-Determination

Belonging — Fun & Enjoyment — Legacy

EMOTIONAL

Secure Privacy — Diminished Stress — Mirroring Values — Appeal by Design — Human Interaction

Health Value — Magnetic Attraction — Accessibility — Helpfulness — Mindfulness

FUNCTIONAL

Reducing Tasks — Long Tail — Simplicity — Income Creation — Reduce Risk — Planning & Order — Puzzle Part

Connects & Excites — Hassle Free — Reduce Cost & Time — Durable Quality — Easy to Understand — Beauty & Balance — Educates & Informs

Pope Francis

A plea for ethical capitalism

Klaus Schwab's plea for humane capitalism has received moral support from no less a person than Pope Francis. The pope has called the business world 'a noble calling, focused on the creation of wealth and making the world a better place'. These are historic words, coming as they do from the leader of a worldwide church. The pope argues for an ethical form of capitalism and an economy on a human scale. In his opinion, this is possible as long as businessmen allow themselves to be guided by their moral compass. To support this process, the Council for Inclusive Capitalism was set up in 2016, an initiative that enjoys the backing, amongst others, of Mastercard, Allianz, Johnson & Johnson, Estée Lauder, Bank of America, Dupont, EY and BP, as well as the United Nations, the OECD and the TUC.

In addition to the Stakeholder Capitalism concept, I am also charmed by the Good Karma AI (Artificial Intelligence) concept proposed by Jonathan Berte, CEO of Robovision in the De Tijd Vooruit podcast. His company has achieved huge international success in the field of AI applications based on visual data. Berte sees it as his mission to democratise AI by making it simpler and more user-friendly, so that access to this new technology can be spread further than the large, capital-rich companies to whom it is currently available. With this in mind, Robovision has developed AI applications for agriculture and horticulture, in which robots help to distinguish good seed and plants from bad ones. Similarly, in the food industry the company has created an AI system for Ritter, to prevent bad nuts from being incorporated into their delicious chocolate bars. The corona crisis also gave a boost to the use of AI software by doctors; for example, for the interpretation of CT scans of the lungs, which allowed the right treatment to be given to COVID patients more quickly. Another promising AI application in the medical world is TrialJectory: software that analyses the data of many thousands of clinical trials for the treatment of cancer, so that the best treatment for each individual patient can be determined.

These are all examples of what Berte calls Good Karma AI, in contrast to Bad Karma AI, examples of which include the applications used by the Chinese government to monitor its people or the software used by the Trump administration to decide which migrants should be forcibly repatriated. With Bad Karma AI, the algorithm is a black box, so that outsiders have no idea of the rules that are used to steer the system's self-learning processes.

If a Zoonotic feels no affinity with Stakeholder Capitalism and Good Karma AI, there is a strong likelihood that it will eventually become a Predator Zoonotic, like Robinhood or Uber.

Is Jonathan Berte's vision no more than an idealistic dream? Perhaps, but it is a dream that a genuine Zoonotic will do its level best to make come true.

ROLE MODEL>
ALEXANDRIA OCASIO-CORTEZ: THE
FACE OF A NEW GENERATION

Another powerful and highly visible example of a Zoonotic leader is undoubtedly Alexandria Ocasio-Cortez. At just 29 years of age, this woman from the Bronx with Puerto Rican roots is the youngest ever person to sit in the American Congress. Since her election, her initials AOC have developed into a strong brand, a political equivalent of the French Appellation d'Origine Contrôlée wine quality label. She now has more than 3.5 million Twitter followers, compared with just 45,000 before the election. She knows from her own experience what it is like to work in the so-called 'gig economy' in the US. The employees in this economy seldom have proper social security status, as is the case, for example, with the drivers and couriers of Uber. And like many other young people in America, she also knows what it is like to be burdened with the huge costs of further education in her country. She began her political career as a volunteer in the Bernie Sanders campaign team, working from door to door to talk with voters in the Bronx and Queens.

TIME Magazine *describes her as 'The Phenomenon' and 'Arguably the best storyteller in the Democratic Party since Barack Obama'.*

She does not think in terms of party interests but in terms of social movements. Likewise, she is not simply interested in winning votes, but wants to capture hearts and minds. She seeks to achieve the best possible rather than the practicably feasible. She thinks in terms of five years or longer. 'By the time legislation actually gets through, it is five years from now,' she says. 'So everything we introduce needs to have 2025 or our kids in mind.' She not only wishes to achieve a majority in Congress for her party for the next few years, but wants to help set the agenda for the coming decades.

I am firmly convinced that the leaders who will make a difference in the future will be those who strive to achieve 'purposeful leadership'. In this context, the keynote given by Ilham Kadri, the CEO of Solvay, during the Annual Global Meeting of Vlerick Alumni touched me deeply. She testified that the first seeds of her interest in sustainability were sown during the years of her youth, when she was raised by her grandmother in a modest family with equally modest resources in Casablanca.

> 'There are two important days in your life: the first is the day you were born; the second is the day when you realise why you were born.'

According to an old African saying used in her country, a girl has only two ways out in life: marriage and death. Ilham says that she discovered a third way: education. She had a passion for scientific research, but also a desire to be part of a wider ecosystem.

As a leader, she sees it as her role to allow the potential of her company and its employees to develop fully, by working together for a meaningful purpose. This purpose starts at the top, but will not work if it is imposed from above: bottom-up engagement is essential. Purpose must be a fundamental and sincerely held part of the company culture, which finds proper expression in its strategy and structures.

> The leader keeps his/her eyes fixed on both the long term (telescopic vision) and the short term (microscopic vision).

She seeks to achieve not simply linear growth, but also holistic growth. Everything begins with the 'why'. At Solvay, this 'why' is 'to reinvent progress for sustainable growth' in three core domains: people, planet and profit (or pocket, as she prefers to call it). 'We act with profound attention to ethics, safety and well-being.' She is proud, for example, that in the United States Solvay is the largest 'solar farmer' in the chemical industry.

As a result of corona, the company now pays more attention than ever before to both sides of the business medal. This finds expression in the importance of the word 'AND'.

'We dare AND we care; we are ambitious AND humble.'

At the end of her impressive and memorable testimony, she concluded by saying that there is now a third and fourth important day in your life: the third is the day that you successfully achieve your meaningful purpose; the fourth is when you help someone else to achieve theirs.

EXPERT OPINION

Jacques Vandermeiren

CEO Port of Antwerp

Sustainability as a mission

'I not only believe in the concept of Stakeholder Capitalism, but am also heavily involved in a number of organisations that actively seek to promote it, such as The Shift (theshift.be), a Belgian collaborative platform for sustainability. Its objective: to achieve with its members and partners the transition to a better society and economy. Its method: Connect. Commit. Change.

In my opinion, the harbour and other public companies like De Lijn bus and tram service have an important pioneering role to play, not least because of their high level of social visibility.

The debate about the expansion of Ineos in the harbour at Antwerp is one of the concrete cases in which the application of Stakeholder Capitalism is being tested: finding the right balance between economic concerns and local, international and ecological problems.

It is probably easier to achieve this kind of transition in family businesses than in stock-quoted, quarterly-driven companies. In these bigger companies the CEO and the board of directors have an added responsibility to ensure movement in the right direction, but this applies equally to the institutional investors in, for example, pension funds.

The COVID-19 crisis is an urgent invitation to drastically rethink our current economic model, along the lines of the Great Reset, the recent initiative of the World Economic Forum (weforum.org/great-reset).

I believe fully in the following quote that I heard at Davos:

'The view from the top should be more than the bottom-line.'

A Zoonotic leader hunts for latent needs

Your chances of becoming a Zoonotic will be greatly increased if you can succeed in finding and then satisfying a dormant, latent need. This means developing a product or service that meets a need that people are not yet fully aware of themselves. In the paper 'Discovering What People Want Before They Do. Building Innovation Platforms with Latent Consumer Needs', Ipsos cited the example of the hydrating shower gel developed by Dove. When this product first came onto the Asian market shortly after the turn of the century, only 3 percent of consumers regarded the hydrating effect as being important. Two years after its launch, this figure had risen to 12 percent. Another well-known example is Yakult, the daily yoghurt drink that improves your body's natural resistance. Or what about the Swiffer, the easy solution for removing dust and dirt without the need for a sponge or mop?

The only way to discover a latent need is by very carefully observing customer behaviour and by asking them the right questions.

A first step is to establish qualitative recognition. This step has a dual purpose:

1. What are the potential, unanswered needs in a particular category?
2. What new needs might arise in this category, taking account of the macro-economic, socio-demographic and technological trends?

The list of ideas that you collect in this way can then be refined through quantitative research. To categorise the latent needs, the Ipsos model makes use of two dimensions. The first dimension determines the extent to which the need is the deciding factor for the customer's current choice; the second determines the extent to which consumer delight can be increased if the need is met. This is expressed visually in the following matrix.

FRAMEWORK FOR DIFFERENT TYPES OF CONSUMER NEEDS

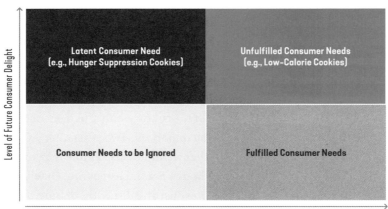

Source: Ipsos

- The blue quadrant: the latent need.
  This need is not yet important in the current choice process, because no one is currently offering a solution, although people would find it great if such a solution existed.
- The red quadrant: the unfulfilled need.
  This need is already important in the current choice process, but has not yet been met. This offers excellent growth opportunities for anyone who can find a solution.
- The light blue quadrant: the fulfilled need.
  This need is also already important in the current choice process but offers little opportunity for growth, since the need has already been met.
- The grey quadrant: the ignored need.
  This need has no influence on the current choice process and therefore also has no impact on customer delight.

The major challenge in finding and identifying a latent need is the very fact of its latency, since this often fails to spontaneously rise to the surface in qualitative studies. Tracking down such needs requires the use of experienced market researchers who know and can employ the right techniques to search for these hidden clumps of gold. It is this kind of latent need that the Zoonotic leader is constantly hoping to find.

INSIGHT

> **The start of a new era**

Like it or not, a new era is dawning for many sectors. This process is inevitable and irreversible. What was previously the exception has become the rule: the internet is now by definition mobile and cars are now by definition self-driving. Electric cars will not only revolutionise the automobile sector, but also associated sectors, such as petrol stations. Or will the electric car already have been overtaken by the hydrogen engine before that happens? Who can say?

Self-driving cars will make it possible for you to travel at 100 kilometres an hour, while you are doing your work in the passenger seat. This will have an enormous impact on our cities and on house prices. Did you know that the arrival of something as seemingly ordinary as the humble bicycle had a positive impact on reducing birth defects in newborn infants, since it made it easier for people to move beyond the limits of their existing gene pool?

The arrival of new crypto applications will have a far-reaching impact comparable to the arrival of the internet.

Machine learning will make it possible to solve certain problems more quickly and more cheaply.

A century ago, China was a political and economic irrelevance for the Western world. Today, its presence and power are dominant around the globe.

ROLE MODEL>
PHILIP INGHELBRECHT: A ZOONOTIC LEADER WITH BELGIAN ROOTS

Philip started his career as an investment banker in Brussels and Luxembourg, but it was his decision to follow an MBA in Berkeley that really changed his life. He had moved to the United States at the start of the 1990s and was so impressed by San Francisco that he promised himself he would one day live and work there. He made good this promise just before the turn of the century, at a moment when the dot.com boom was at its height. Even though he did not have a technology background, he decided to set up a tech company. This was nothing abnormal at that time; everyone was doing it! Together with a fellow student from Berkeley, he hit upon the concept for Shazam at the end of 1999. At first sight, it was not an earth-shattering idea: most of us ask ourselves at least once a day who it was that sang the song we have just heard on the radio. However, the spark of innovation was provided by his business partner, who came up with the plan to link the service they wanted to offer to the telephone. Of course, at that time the mobile phone as we now know it had not yet been invented: the iPhone was only launched in 2007. As a result, Philip and his partners had to wait for more than five years for a Superspreader that could really help their business to skyrocket.

'Technology is something that you need to continuously develop, even if for no other reason than this is what the consumer may or may not latently expect.'

Even today, fifteen years later, the development team at Shazam still contains a dozen or so PhDs, simply to ensure that the technology can continue to be further improved.

Inghelbrecht stepped out of the operational structure of the company in 2004. His latest business venture, Tatari, focuses on the measuring and optimisation of television advertising. Tatari helps its customers to position their TV commercials as ideally as possible and to match them to their potential target public. This is made possible in part by the chips that are nowadays included in every new television set and can register what viewers are watching at any given moment, information that is linked to an (anonymous) IP address. Tatari has only been in business for the past two years, but already employs some 25 personnel. It aims its service primarily at companies that buy advertising time on TV – a market that in the US alone is worth 70 billion dollars – but it is also starting to target television broadcasters as well.

'Technology makes it easier for every entrepreneur to start up a business, but the patterns of expectation in the tech sector are higher, so that the threshold for attracting capital is also that much higher.'

A Zoonotic leader makes use of machine learning

By making smart use of machine learning, the Zoonotic leader succeeds in optimising the ROI on his marketing investment. This should focus primarily on communication via mobile channels (smartphone, tablet, etc.), because by 2025 it is estimated that 62 percent of consumers will be Millennials or even younger: in other words, the mobile generations who have never known anything else.

Machine learning can also be useful when it comes to deciding upon relevant content for your target groups. It helps marketing experts to separate good YouTube videos from bad ones. Creative ideas will continue to be the crucial differentiating factor, but by gaining insights into the deeper patterns underlying consumer behaviour, machine learning can help to optimise the impact of your creative message.

INSIGHT

› What marketeers can learn from chess

Just consider what is happening in the world of chess computers. AlphaGo Zero beat AlphaGo by 100 games to 8. AlphaGo Zero also beat Stockfish by 20 games to 0, and this after Stockfish had already gained 1,000 points more than Magnus Carlsen, the youngest ever world chess champion, who has an IQ of 190. What's more, this trend shows no signs of stopping. In 2020, the newest computer, Leela Chess Zero, played more than 300 million times against itself, simply in order to learn. In short, machine learning is a never-ending game. In future, comparable algorithms will also cause a similar seismic shift in the world of marketing and advertising.

Nicolas Darveau-Garneau is Google's Chief Evangelist. He predicts that by 2025 the sale of media space will be fully automated. According to him, this can increase the return on TV advertising by 160 percent. Or as he puts it:

> 'Automated brand advertising is here to stay,
> without asking your taste for it.'

The five crucial rules for scoring are:

1. Measure the combined effect of the different channels, because, for example, your YouTube campaign will also have an impact on your search results, and vice versa.

2. Optimise your target. Instead of just selling more policies, it is smarter for an insurance company to primarily sell more policies to good risks who are likely to submit significantly fewer damage claims.

3. Optimise your metrics. What metrics are you using: fixed budget, percentage of turnover or ROI? ROI can sometimes be misleading, because an investment of 100,000 euros with a return of 2 million euros results in an ROI of 20:1, while an investment of 10 million euros with a return of 50 million euros only equates to an ROI of 5:1.

4. Optimise for the long term. Those with the highest lifetime value (LTV) will be able to attract the most customers. Amazon customers, for example, have a very high LTV.
5. Attract the best customers. Do not focus on newlyweds, who will only take a single cruise and then stop, but on 'jaggers' (young, active pensioners) who take three cruises a year.

In brand marketing, the emphasis is increasingly being placed on performance marketing, precisely because everything is now so easily measurable and because machine learning makes it possible to bring the invisible underlying patterns in these measurements to the surface. In the world of online advertising, it is important to innovate continually. Adhering to the following three principles will help you to achieve this:

1. Leverage machine learning: make optimal use of all relevant automation tools. It will yield better results, speed up the process and ensure that your marketing investment achieves a consistent ROI.
2. Invest primarily in the customer journey: break through the silos between search, display, video. Invest everywhere where you think your customer needs to hear or see you, providing it is cost-effective. This holistic approach has a positive effect on the return of your strategy.
3. Focus on the right results: look first and foremost at the general evolution of your turnover and not simply at the efficiency of your media. In the long run this will give better overall results and help you to acquire a bigger market share.

A Zoonotic leader sees everything more clearly

Like the Cheetah, a Zoonotic leader has clear vision and sharp focus. He/she looks at things from a different perspective to others. This immediately makes me think of the famous TV commercial by Apple, which used images of great thinkers of recent times, such as Albert Einstein, Bob Dylan, Martin Luther King Jr., Richard Branson, John Lennon, Buckminster Fuller, Thomas Edison, Muhammad Ali, Ted Turner, Maria Callas, Mahatma Gandhi and others, accompanied by this inspirational voice-over:

'Here's to the crazy ones. The misfits. The rebels. The troublemakers. The round pegs in the square holes. The ones who see things differently. They're not fond of rules. And they have no respect for the status quo. You can quote them, disagree with them, glorify or vilify them. About the only thing you can't do is ignore them. Because they change things. They invent. They imagine. They heal. They explore. They create. They inspire. They push the human race forwards. Maybe they have to be crazy.

How else can you stare at an empty canvas and see a work of art? Or sit in silence and hear a song that's never been written? Or gaze at a red planet and see a laboratory on wheels?

We make tools for these kinds of people.
While some see them as the crazy ones, we see genius. Because the people who are crazy enough to think they can change the world, are the ones who do.'

ONE MORE THING

DELIVERECT: MANAGING TAKE-AWAY EFFICIENTLY

Even before the corona pandemic broke out, Zhong Xu and Jan Hollez were convinced that takeaway offered excellent growth opportunities. Thanks to Posios, their successful cash register system for the catering industry, they already had significant experience of the sector. However, what the restaurant and bar owners were lacking was a single common interface. If you cannot sell your products and services via multiple channels, it becomes difficult to survive.

A restaurant can generate additional turnover via online sales, but the operational functioning still needs to be managed through your cash register. With this in mind, Zhong developed Deliverect, which makes it possible for restaurant and bar owners worldwide to link their cash register to the IT systems of various meal providers. As a result, corona was able to create exponential growth. By the middle of 2020, they had already had more than 10 million orders for the system.

SWEETIE EXPOSES PAEDOPHILES

Child sex tourism is a disgusting and deeply deplorable problem worldwide. The international child help organisation Terre des Hommes, working together with the Dutch advertising bureau Lemz, has developed a smart idea to put the brakes on so-called webcam sex tourism. In 2013, they created the profile of a 10-year-old virtual Philippine girl as a lure to expose child abusers. To find out exactly how a child can be abused via a webcam, the researchers went undercover to join various chatrooms. The virtual girl was given the name 'Sweetie', a name that often crops up in chatrooms of this kind. In just two months, Sweetie had had online conversations with more than a thousand men. In this way, they were able to identify more than a thousand predatory males and were able to record them on video.

A follow-up project saw the arrival of Sweetie 2.0. According to the FBI, there are unquestionably still a large number of internet sites where men go in search of webcam sex. Sweetie 2.0 conducts conversations with these men via chat rooms with the help of a chatbot. This means that Sweetie 2.0 can use a number of different profiles and can have a dozen or so different conversations at the same time.

As you might expect, the conversations were not of a high intellectual level, but this was not necessary, since not many of Sweetie's conversation 'partners' spoke good English. Once again, more than a thousand child abusers in 71 different countries were exposed. Terre des Hommes and psychologists believe that this hard confrontational method will help to bring about a reduction in the level of abuse.

1. What is the creative idea and who benefits from it?

The brain behind the idea is Mark Woerde of the Dutch advertising bureau Lemz. He has already drawn his inspiration for a number of years from what he calls 'goodvertising'. He developed the campaign for Terre des Hommes and won five Golden Lions in Cannes in three different categories: PR, Direct and Promo-activation.

2. What makes it possible for the idea to be shared? What are the memorable buzzwords or hashtags?

The press conference for the launch of Sweetie was breaking news worldwide. During the launch, Interpol was presented with a file containing the details of more than a thousand child abusers. As a result, the problem was immediately put on the political and social agenda in countless countries.

3. How can you use time pressure to accelerate the speed of development?

In view of the seriousness of the problem, a fast approach made a huge difference for thousands of innocent children worldwide.

4. How do you get the support of big names and how do you find a match with important influencers?

Sweetie had no need of influencers. It was credible enough to lure child abusers into the trap. Mark Woerde has now become an influencer himself in the world of advertising. He challenges his colleagues to tackle diverse social problems with creative solutions. He does not necessarily mean the world's very largest problems, such as war or world peace, but also less visible yet equally serious problems, such as loneliness. This was the challenge that Nathalie Erdmanis, Director of Strategic Marketing at the AG insurance company, decided to tackle in collaboration with the Air advertising agency. When the curve of the corona pandemic began to flatten out, so that the lockdown measures could gradually be relaxed, people began to hope that it would soon be possible to return to a more or less 'normal' social life. However, for far too many lonely men, women and children in Belgium the improved medical situation promised to bring little change.

A study conducted by the University of Ghent revealed that in 2018 – in other words, before the pandemic – 46 percent of the population admitted to having feelings of loneliness. For them, the atmosphere of the lockdown would continue. AG believes that these people must not be forgotten, now that the crisis is passing. With the help of Air, they launched a solidarity campaign that encourages the fortunate majority to give up a little of their time to support the organisations that try to combat loneliness in the field. In concrete terms, this involved the creation of a website – allentegen-eenzaamheid.be – that offered practical advice for the lonely and those who wish to help them. What can we do each day? What organisations are looking for volunteers? What can you do if you are feeling lonely? Why is it important both to give and to receive help?

5. How can you use a memorable and compact video?

Mark Woerde and his colleagues at Lemz approached the problem in a manner that was radically different from anything that had ever gone before. They first carried out in-depth research into the problem, so that they could understand it from top to bottom. They conducted interviews with the best experts from several relevant sectors, from the police and the legal profession to ICT, but also spoke to dozens of child victims through the intercession of social workers in the Philippines. It became clear that the real problem was that hardly anyone filed complaints against the offenders, so that the police were powerless to take action, even though they knew that hundreds of criminal acts were being committed each day. It was therefore necessary to bring about a change from reactive to proactive tracing of these offenders. Enter Sweetie, a computer-controlled 3D model.

Talk about a memorable video! She was certainly memorable for the child abusers she deceived. This proves that when technology, creativity and ethics work together, they can change the world for the better.

6. How does the campaign motivate and demonstrate both engagement and altruism?

Initially, Lemz developed the campaign without publicity in a secluded warehouse. It was only after they had been active for a year that the agency finally came out of the shadows and stepped into the limelight. Not with the intention of harvesting praise, but rather to show their colleagues in the advertising world that it is possible, with the necessary creativity, to make a real difference in people's lives, even for a delicate subject like child pornography. In this way, Mark Woerde wanted to pass on the Zoonotic baton to others.

7. How can you ensure that the threshold to participate is as low as possible?

More than 1 billion people saw the Sweetie campaign and more than half a million signed the petition, which puts pressure on the authorities in the countries concerned to provide better protection for their children. Webcam sex tourism is recognised as a problem worldwide and the Philippine police regard it as a serious crime. By influencing public opinion and the international agenda, police forces have more possibilities and bigger budgets to fight child abuse.

3

DEVELOP AN AGILE ZOONOTIC TEAM

It should be obvious that a successful viral business strategy is only possible through fantastic team work. Because of the complexity of the challenges, more than ever before, you now need a team with a multi-disciplinary and, preferably, even a multi-cultural background. Search above all for people who are not only good at their job, but are also good for your company culture.

Give the young cubs a chance

If you are looking to find a Zoonotic leader in your company, be prepared to give your younger employees a chance. Sadly, this is not always the case. A study by Glassdoor in the US, UK, France and Germany showed that young employees (aged between 18 and 34) have a greater likelihood of experiencing age discrimination than older employees (55+). In the first age group, 52 percent feel that they are not always given the recognition they deserve, against 39 percent in the second group. Emma Waldman reached the same conclusion in the *Harvard Business Review*, where she described the same phenomenon as 'reverse ageism'. Young people feel that older people look down on them, giving them tasks that are not really challenging and generally showing them few signs of trust and confidence.

Whereas in reality it is precisely these young cubs – the young Cheetahs in my imaginary world – who have the drive, the flexibility and the lack of preconceptions that are so important for the success of a Zoonotic strategy.

How to win the trust of your young people

Because of their relative youth, Zoonotic leaders sometimes have less experience and therefore seem less credible to more experienced team members. On the reverse side of the coin, they are always bursting with energy. If you are a young Cheetah leader, you can overcome this lack of confidence in you by taking the following actions.

1. Empower your team members

In the beginning, your team members will probably be a little wary of you. As a result, your opinion will often be questioned. This makes it essential that you should first and foremost learn as much as you can about the industry and the organisation in which you work. This will allow you to answer the doubters with concrete facts and figures, rather than with misplaced self-confidence.

Acquiring knowledge takes time. Consequently (and paradoxically), this means that you will first have to give your team trust before you can expect them to trust you. Avoid taking authoritarian decisions and give your people the necessary space to make their own choices. This will increase their engagement with the team. If people feel involved in the decision-making process, they are more prepared to support the final outcome, whatever that outcome might be.

> 'Treating people as capable adults shows you trust them to be part of good decisions. They'll trust you more in return.'
> **ANDY ATKINS**

2. Embrace curiosity

According to a study carried out by PricewaterhouseCoopers, curiosity is one of the most important qualities for future leaders. Michael Dell goes even further: the founder of the computer giant believes that curiosity is the single most important quality for success in the years ahead. Although curiosity is crucial for leaders of all ages, it is doubly crucial for young leaders. It challenges them to overcome their lack of knowledge and to strengthen their relations with their older and more experienced team members. Questioning, listening and learning: that is the key. And do not be afraid to admit that there are some things you do not know. Daring to show your vulnerability is a sign of maturity and curiosity.

Richard Branson is the prototype of a curiosity-driven leader. He launched *Student Magazine* when he was just 16 years old. By the time he was 20, he had started a record company. In his autobiography he says that he named his company Virgin because he and all his colleagues were virgins in the business world.

'The future belongs to the curious – don't be afraid to ask questions and see where your curiosity takes you.'
RICHARD BRANSON

When he is recruiting new personnel, Philip Inghelbrecht does not use standard interview techniques. 'In interviews you meet lots of good candidates. The problem is that you only find out a couple of months later whether or not they are really as good as you thought. So I do things differently. My candidates are given a mass of homework before they get to see me. That way, I can know if they are really top-notch. If they are not prepared to make the effort, they don't get in.' You need to search for people who see lack of control as an opportunity, not as a hindrance.

3. Trust passion

Passion is not just a frivolous slogan of the Millennials. Research by Deloitte has shown that passionate team members are twice as innovative. They perform better because of their greater internal drive to continue learning and growing. Passion is the most distinguishing quality of a Zoonotic leader. Your passion not only feeds your own desire for learning and growth, but also inspires your team members to push their own boundaries. Jennifer Hyman was just 29 years old when she started Rent the Runway, a website where you can hire designer clothes. Although at first her idea was rejected by various designers, her limitless passion allowed her to persist in the pursuit of her dream. Today, she has more than 1,800 people working for her company, which is worth almost 1 billion dollars.

This is the advice of Philip Inghelbrecht: 'My first question to someone who approaches me with an idea is always this: "Are you also doing something else at the moment, or is this the only thing that interests you?" It is only if they answer "yes" to the second part of this question that our conversation will continue. For a start-up, it really is a matter of all or nothing. During my start-up period, I had no house, no wife, no family and not even a dog! As a result, my fixed costs were low and I wasn't running much of a risk. My advice? If you want to start a company, do it before you are thirty. Your risk profile at that age is completely different from what it will become later on.'

In their book *The Secret of Silicon Valley*, the Dutch authors Eva Schram and Wibe Wagemans write that 'grit' is one of the key characteristics of many of the tech entrepreneurs in the Valley. They define this as a combination of determination and passion: you refuse to allow yourself to be knocked off course by setbacks, because you are 200 percent convinced that your idea is a winner. 'Cognitive ability is just one of the many characteristics that are necessary to help people become successful in Silicon Valley. Just being smart or having a great idea or thinking big will not get you very far. Yes, ambition is important. Yes, openness and collaboration are the cornerstones of the innovation ecosystem in the Valley. But if you really want to make it in the Valley, you have got to have grit,' say Schram and Wagemans. The cover of their book carries a quote by Walter De Brouwer, a Belgian tech entrepreneur and professor at Stanford University: 'Europe tanks on diesel; the Valley tanks on rocket fuel'. To which Wagemans later adds: 'My passion in life is figuring out exactly how consumers use new technologies. Building products and brands, bringing them to market, stimulating their use: that is what the running of my start-up involves, each and every day. Leadership, team spirit and growth are the result, but I also have a huge amount of fun, irrespective of how many zeroes are tacked on to the end of the turnover figures.'

A start-up is a bit like a child: if things are
not going right somewhere – for example, at school –
you need to invest more time.

EXPERT OPINION

Angela Lee Duckworth

University of Pennsylvania

Grit makes the difference

When I look at the many Zoonotic leaders I know, I think spontaneously of the TED Talk given by Angela Lee Duckworth, a psychologist who studies in particular why some students, notwithstanding their high IQ, score less well or give up more easily than other students who are less mentally gifted.

In her opinion, the answer is 'grit'.

Grit = Passion + Perseverance

'People with grit,' says Duckworth, 'have a strong belief that they can grow and continue learning, so that failure is not a permanent condition.' To my way of thinking, that is precisely a key characteristic of a successful Zoonotic leader. According to Professor Scott Galloway, it was precisely because of a lack of grit that the streaming service Quibi ended in failure. In spite of all the initial enthusiasm at its launch, the company turned out to be an empty box. Galloway contends that no successful media-tech company has ever been set up by people over the age of sixty. Why? 'The young brain is crazy, creative and willing to work 80 hours a week, because young people think that they will live forever. People in their sixties are not blessed/cursed with any of these things, which makes them decent leaders, great mentors and shitty entrepreneurs.'

Apart from entrepreneurial drive, Schram and Wagemans argue that there are two other key factors that explain the success of Silicon Valley: the availability of venture capitalists with knowledge of the sector and the numerous networks that are prepared to share information with each other. A good idea is just 1 percent success; the rest is hard work. In *Knack* magazine the authors advised budding entrepreneurs to think like Elon Musk, who prides himself on the fact that he never takes on new ventures blindly: he always asks the 'why' question, which always leads him to the fundamental building blocks for success.

Empowerment, curiosity and passion: those are the three vital characteristics that a Zoonotic leader must possess if he/she wants to build a strong and agile Zoonotic team.

4. Cultivate the 'pay it forward' principle

According to Wagemans, the Valley works on the basis of the 'pay it forward' principle. This means that you pass on to others the same kind of help and learning experiences that you have received in the past. In other words, instead of 'pay it back' – doing something for the people who have done something for you – you 'pay it forward' – doing something for others who can benefit from what you have learned. Without this principle, the Valley would be a very different place, says Wagemans. 'I have been able to build my career in a number of adventurous places, including six countries where I lived with my family. Even though I have been able as a serial entrepreneur to develop start-ups and corporates in North and Latin America, Europe, Asia and Australia, there is still one place that stands head and shoulders above the rest: Silicon Valley. Even if you are setting up a non-profit organisation – for example, to make a contribution towards equal opportunities for all children in America or for the preservation of nature – the lessons of the Valley are of huge value.'

Go for a truly fab team

In *De Tijd* newspaper Fons Van Dyck wrote an inspirational article, in which he argued that any company that hopes to survive in the long term needs to put together a diverse and complementary team of explorers, conquerors, connectors and defenders. His article appeared in response to the formation of the Vivaldi coalition in Belgium, whose new prime minister, Alexander De Croo, cited a quote by basketball legend Michael Jordan:

'Talent wins games.
Teamwork wins championships.'

Advice from the CFO of Google

When I was a guest at Googleplex, the headquarters of Google in California, amongst the people I met was their CFO, Ruth Porat, a truly inspirational woman who made a huge impression on me. She emphasised that we are still too lax when it comes to our approach to avoidable problems. 'Every day, as many people are dying on our roads as in a plane crash with a Boeing 747. Similarly, medical error is the third most common cause of death. These are at least two key areas where AI can make a big difference.' Her advice to companies is:

1. Map out the areas in which you are vulnerable.
2. Invest with the long term in mind. 'You can't cost cut your way to innovation.'
3. Continue to invest in training and in bold 'moonshot' ideas that can change the world.
4. Never stop searching for the right people for your team. 'Find them, grow them, keep them.'
5. Focus above all on things that can speed up your processes.

According to Van Dyck, it is a good idea as a leader to allow yourself to be inspired by the example of The Beatles. 'Steve Jobs, the founder of Apple, was once asked to explain his business model. Many people thought that he would attribute the company's success to Apple's superior technology or the user-friendliness of its products, or the iconic appeal of the Apple brand, or even his own charismatic leadership. But no, he didn't. Instead he referred to The Beatles as his ultimate role model. They were four strong individuals, each with their own distinct character and personality. At times, this led to tension and even confrontation. But as long as they kept everything in balance, The Beatles continued to be greater than the sum of John, Paul, George and Ringo as individuals. "Great things," concluded Jobs, "are never the result of a single person, but of a group of people". Coming from a super-ego like Steve Jobs, this speaks volumes. When The Beatles split after ten years and went their separate ways, none of them ever had the same meteoric success they had enjoyed as when they were the Fab Four.

In enlightened management circles there has been a realisation for a number of years that the most successful teams are diverse teams. For this reason, companies now strive to achieve not only gender equality, but also cultural diversity. But even more important is the need to consciously create teams that are also diverse in terms of the leadership styles they contain.

To guarantee that a team can adjust quickly in a rapidly changing VUCA (volatile, uncertain, complex, ambiguous) environment, it must have first and foremost a number of explorers. These are people who have a very broad view of the world and are far ahead of their time. They sense as few others can that the world is changing and want to change with it.

Explorers are sometimes dismissed as visionary dreamers who lack decisiveness. For this reason, it is also important for a strong team to have a number of conquerors, to whom the development of strategy and the realisation of objectives can be entrusted.. The conquerors are very ambitious and concentrate on results. They want their company, brand, country, etc. to win. "Getting things done" is their mantra.

Both these leadership profiles have an extreme focus on the outside world. They often experience the internal organisation of their company as a brake on progress and a hindrance to what they want to achieve. Consequently, they will try to change the internal culture or even destroy it, in their restless pursuit of innovation and improvement. However, they often run into a brick wall of resistance and frequently need to accept setbacks.

This explains why a company also needs connectors. These are people who are able to build bridges both internally and externally with customers and other stakeholders. They are diplomats who dislike conflict. Instead, they search for allies both inside and outside the company. As a result, they are able to keep everything together and moving in the right direction.

Last but not least, an organisation that wishes to survive in the long term will need a number of defenders. They guarantee the identity, culture and values of the company. Their preference is for evolution, not revolution. They understand better than anyone else that a smart and sensitive approach to culture, whether of the company or of an entire country, is the most crucial key to sustainable success.

These four profiles are very different, but at the same time they are also complementary. If the four profiles can manage to work together, success is guaranteed. By collaborating across boundaries and sensitivities, they will be able to ensure survival, whilst also remaining true to who they are.'

I am firmly of the opinion that as a Zoonotic leader you need to be the John Lennon in your team; the explorer of whom Fons Van Dyck says: 'These are people who have a very broad view of the world and are far ahead of their time. They sense as few others can that the world is changing and want to change with it.'

Big Hairy Audacious Goals as the binder

BHAGs (Big Hairy Audacious Goals) first became known thanks to the bestseller *Built to Last* by Jim Collins and Jerry Porras. According to their definition: 'A BHAG is clear and compelling and serves as a unifying point on which all efforts can be focused, as a result of which an intense team spirit is often created. It has a clear finishing line, so that everyone in the organisation knows when the goal has been reached. People must be able to understand it immediately, without the need for much explanation.'

In this context, Wibe Wagemans has commented: 'I always take the necessary time to formulate the right BHAG, having first considered all the alternatives. The simplicity and focus of a BHAG often has a contagious effect on people, which creates support for all the various strategies that can help to achieve it. The BHAG is not a vision; it is a concrete objective that you wish to reach by a fixed date in the short or medium term. It is by no means self-evident that everyone in the company will immediately see its strategic relevance or become inspired by it. This is why you need to start an internal buy-in process. Take the time to explain the BHAG to your team and check that they understand it. Everyone, without exception, must be willing and able to commit to it. It is not always easy to choose a BHAG that is as clear and compelling as a "moonshot", but it is worth making the effort to try. You will be amazed just how inspirational big objectives can be.'

Ensure connection

Creative people love freedom. No one knows this better than Netflix, a company that does much more than simply pay lip service to the idea. This is what Wibe Wagemans and Eva Schram had to say on the matter: 'Reed Hastings founded the company in 1997 based on the idea of "people over process". Hastings believes that people perform best if they are given freedom and responsibility. This involves, amongst other things, that employees at Netflix are allowed an unlimited number of days annual leave (something that is also the case in many other Valley companies) and can submit expenses claims without the approval of their managers. There is also no limit to the number of days maternity/paternity leave they can take, with most taking between four and eight months. "You might perhaps think that this kind of freedom leads to chaos," says the company website, "but it doesn't. We don't have a dress code either, but so far nobody has come to work naked. You don't need a policy for everything. People understand the advantages of wearing clothes if you are going to work." In The Netherlands, the AFAS software company has a similar philosophy, which CEO Bas van der Veldt summarised in an interview for the Ondernemer website as: "Working with common sense in the interests of AFAS".

So does freedom of this kind never lead to abuse? Of course it does. In his book *No Rules Rules*, Hastings cites the example of a Taiwanese employee who claimed 100,000 dollars for luxury trips that had nothing to do with Netflix. When this was discovered after three years, the employee was, unsurprisingly, sacked. However, Hastings added that this did not deter him from continuing to offer his people huge amounts of freedom, because for a creative company the loss of innovation that would result from less freedom is a much bigger risk to take.'

EXPERT OPINION

Peter Somers
CEO Emirates Post

No business transformation without a viral transformation of the company culture

I know Peter for the time when we worked together for the Belgian postal service, bpost. He is currently working in Dubai as the CEO of Emirates Post. I have great respect and admiration for Peter, not only because of his wide experience in e-commerce logistics and retail, but also because of his communication style. As a leader, he succeeds even in the most trying circumstances in improving the performance of his team and his company. Peter accepted the difficult challenge of transforming Emirates Post from a state-run public company to a modern, productive and agile postal company with strong international ambitions.

In our Zoom conversation, he emphasised that a business transformation also demands a viral transformation of the company culture and a radical change in the behaviour of the company's personnel. Exactly how you approach these delicate matters depends, according to Peter, on the nature of the current culture and the current condition of the company. In a relatively mature company, this can probably be achieved via a specific multi-centric approach that makes use of the necessary viral change agents. These are inserted at crucial positions throughout the organisation on the basis of non-hierarchical authority. By aiming for a high degree of connectivity and trust, these change agents seek to change people's general behaviour. As such, they are one of the catalysts for the change process.

However, in a more autocratic business culture – of the type often found in state-run enterprises or more traditional family companies – this kind of 'softly, softly' approach is unlikely to be immediately successful. In part, this is because of the historic inertia experienced by employees in these organisations over many years. In such instances, a top-down approach in which management listens carefully to and communicates clearly with the workforce is more appropriate. This is the approach that Peter quickly initiated soon after his appointment, focusing on a very clear internal communication strategy that included CEO newsflashes, CEO videos, CEO top 100 meetings, CEO roadshows and 'coffee-with-the-CEO' sessions, during which he listened to the concerns of small groups of employees. Running parallel with this communication campaign, it was also crucial in this phase to issue clear, concrete and unambiguous instructions about the changes that were needed.

Peter started this approach at the top, with the senior management, before working his way down layer by layer through the organisation. This was a delicate exercise, where the right balance needed to be constantly found between an empathic and a more directive management style. As an additional complication, Peter also had to deal with the 50 different nationalities that Emirates Post employs, each with their own culture and behavioural preferences. This made the creation of a clear and uniform company culture all the more difficult.

At the moment he is still engaged in the top-down phase of his strategy, awaiting the right moment to switch to the 'viral change' phase that will bring about the completion of the transformation that is needed. One of the initiatives that he is introducing this year to support this process is the 'Great Place to Work' programme. This strategic programme is designed to demonstrate the added value of also investing in the company's people, not only in its systems and structures. According to Peter, a company's human capital is its largest and most valuable asset. The 'Great Place to Work' concept has the further advantage of providing a well-developed roadbook with the necessary KPIs and research to evaluate the continued progress of the transformation.

In addition, he will shortly roll out a digital micro-learning experience platform, which will deal with the necessary challenges in terms of the company's skill gaps. However, its main benefit, in Peter's eyes, is the simplicity of the platform and the way in which it will enhance the communication of change throughout the organisation. Not only in terms of giving clear direction, but also in terms of increasing engagement and facilitating feedback. As a result, the impact of his various initiatives can be measured faster and easier.

It should be evident that the viral transformation of an organisation's culture seldom progresses exponentially but takes time and requires a specific approach, especially in these corona-infected times.

Search for team members beyond your own national borders

According to Bart Decrem, a Belgian entrepreneur in Silicon Valley, it is possible that the corona pandemic will turn out to be a real game-changer, because the huge increase in working from home means that the connective pull provided by the physical location of the Valley has become looser during the past year and a half. As a result, the playing field for the rest of the world in relation to the Valley will become increasingly level. Or to express it in the worlds of Walter De Brouwer, a Belgian professor at Stanford University: 'Silicon Valley is on the way to becoming more an idea than a location'.

In a blogpost on FlexJobs, Emily Courtney describes how 29 important companies, in part as a result of the corona crisis, now see remote teamwork as their standard form of work, which means that people all around the world can collaborate with each other from the comfort of their own front rooms. The results of a study carried out by Global Workplace Analytics confirmed that 86 percent of people working together in this way experience the process as being highly productive. Of the 3,000 respondents, 76 percent said that in future they want to work from home for at least two and a half days each week. You can find a list of the 29 companies – which not only includes the 'usual suspects' like Facebook and Amazon – and their varying approaches on https://www.flexjobs.com/blog/post/companies-switching- remote-work-long-term/.

THE ICE BUCKET CHALLENGE: OR HOW A COLD SHOWER HELPED IN THE FIGHT AGAINST ALS

This campaign was mentioned more than 2 billion times online and was viewed across the world by more than 440 million people. According to Facebook Newsroom, which monitored Facebook traffic and content relating to the Ice Bucket Challenge, between 1 June and 1 September 2014 more than 15 million Ice Bucket videos were shared on the platform. The Challenge ultimately raised 41.8 million dollars for the ALS Association in the US. Moreover, there was also a spill-over effect to other countries, as a result of which the ALS Society in Canada received 26 million dollars during the same period, with the Motor Neurone Disease Association receiving 7 million and the ALS Foundation in The Netherlands, 1 million.

1. What is the creative idea and who benefits from it?

In August 2014, the Ice Bucket Challenge was a viral hit on various social media channels. Facebook, Twitter and Instagram were flooded with videos in which people allowed a bucket of ice-cold water to be poured over their head. This creative challenge was devised by the American ALS Association to raise awareness for this deadly muscular disease, whilst at the same time raising funds for research to combat its effects and find a cure.

2. What stimulates people to share the idea?

The task was simple and contained a double challenge: first to let the water be poured over your head and then to nominate someone else for the same treatment. This was the motor for the viral effect.

3. How can you use time pressure to speed up the process?

People were given just 24 hours to let themselves be dowsed and to pass on the challenge to the next 'victim'. If you refused or failed, you were expected to make a donation to the ALS Association.

4. How do you get the support of big names?

The campaign moved into overdrive when the professional golfer Greg Norman challenged Matt Lauer, the news anchor of *NBC Today*. Talk show host Ellen DeGeneres soon joined in the fun and even Kim Kardashian allowed herself to be soaked for a good cause. DeGeneres donated a large sum to ALS research and her example and the example of other influencers with a large fan base sparked off the Challenge's exponential growth.

5. How can you use short and memorable videos?

The shock effect of seeing someone you know waiting in trepidation to have a bucket of ice-cold water poured over his/her head, followed by the resultant screams and laughter, was an infectious combination. The images were both dramatic and comic, and left no one unmoved. What's more, social media platforms like Facebook, Twitter and LinkedIn like videos of this kind and use their algorithms to push them even harder.

6. How does your campaign motivate altruism?

The Ice Bucket Challenge made it easy to demonstrate your kind heart. It was a challenge in which you had to be prepared literally and metaphorically to 'take the plunge'.

7. How can you ensure that the threshold to participate is as low as possible?

A smartphone and a bucket of water was all you needed to take part in the Ice Bucket Challenge. This low threshold and the fact that you could select the next 'victim' strengthened the viral effect.

4

WORK AT DEVELOPING YOUR OWN ZOONOTIC STRATEGY

The moment has come to roll up your sleeves and get started: in this chapter, the focus is on action! Developing your own Zoonotic is something of a leap in the dark. Sadly, I cannot give you a ready-made recipe for success in your circumstances. All I can do is encourage you and inspire you to implement various brainstormings, reflection sessions and processes that will take you and your team out of your comfort zone. This is something that you have to do for yourself. I cannot do it for you, although I am certainly available to offer you all the support I can give.

As my coach once said to me, during my preparation for a marathon, when he unveiled his proposed training schedule:

> 'If you follow this schedule, there is a
> good chance that you will reach the finishing line,
> but you will have to do it all yourself.'

In the following pages I offer you a wide range of exercises that can help. I have used them myself and I know that they can lead to the most surprising results. At the start of each exercise, I indicate how much time you will need; the optimal group size; the level of complexity; the extent to which you will need to leave your comfort zone; and the materials you will require. These exercises follow a more or less logical order, in the sense that the earlier ones are also the easier ones. As you proceed, you will find them more complex and more probing.

The best way to prepare yourself to meet
a Zoonotic attack is to think about how you might
also become a Zoonotic.

Exercise 1: The hot-air balloon

This exercise is inspired by Thales Macedo of Hyper Island. We take an imaginary journey across the savannah in a balloon, searching for a safe oasis with a healing spring that can save us. We use the balloon as a metaphor to identify our strengths, weaknesses, external forces, stakeholders and goals. The fun thing about this exercise is that you don't need to wrestle with a complex (and often boring!) matrix, but instead you take a journey that challenges you to throw away all your familiar frames of reference. We survey the savannah, see our Cheetahs (= Unfair Advantages) and try to spot the obstacles and threats in their path.

> STEP 1: WIND

These are all the external forces that can have an influence on the course of our balloon – both opportunities and threats. For example, legal, social and/or technological changes over which we have no control.

> STEP 2: SANDBAGS

These are our internal threats and weaknesses, which can slow us or even bring us down.

> STEP 3: HOT AIR

These are all the strengths of our organisation: our service, our products, our culture, our values, our insights into and our connection with the trends that are active in society, as well as all other factors over which we have control and which together ensure that we have an Unfair Advantage.

> STEP 4: PASSENGERS

These are all our internal stakeholders who have an influence on the direction of our balloon and who must prevent us from becoming the target of a Zoonotic attack.

> STEP 5: OBSERVERS

These are all the target groups and users of our products and services who we wish to defend and preserve, as well as all our external stakeholders who, like us, have an interest in our survival and future success.

> STEP 6: WATER IN THE SAVANNAH

This is our dream, the ultimate destination towards which we are travelling and which we hope to reach within a period of 36 to 60 months. What does our future look like in our imagination?

> STEP 7: STEP-BY-STEP PLAN

These are the measures that we need to take along our way across the savannah, so that we can reach the life-giving water.

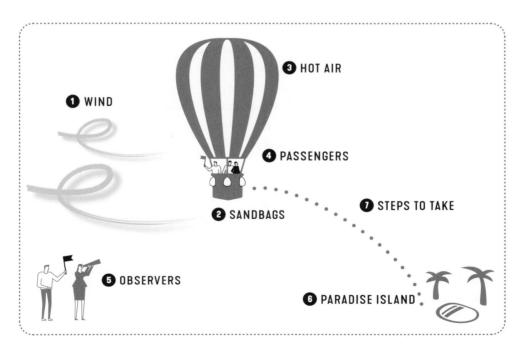

Exercise 2: Reflecting on the spread of innovations

For this exercise it is important that all the participants are familiar with the dead option curve of Everett M. Rogers, which illustrates the different stages in the spreading of innovations. The intention is that the participants think about the phase in which their company is currently positioned: innovator, early adopter, early majority, late majority or laggard? You can also use this model to look at your own staff and to likewise ask in which stage they currently find themselves. Becoming a Zoonotic will be a much harder challenge for the late majority and the laggards than for the innovators.

You need to think about why, how and at what speed innovations spread in your company culture. What channels and social systems play a role in this process? When and how can you reach your critical mass?

Insights into the innovation curve are necessary both to develop your own Zoonotic strategy and to defend yourself against external Zoonotic attack.

> STEP 1: TAPE-IT
Mark out the innovation curve on the floor with some tape. Make the curve sufficiently large, so that you can add in the different stages.

> STEP 2: PROJECT-IT
Project a slide with an image of the model and give a description of the significance of each different stage. These descriptions can be short; the curve is only intended to stimulate the reflective process.

> STEP 3: ASK-IT
Ask the participants to think briefly about the following five questions:
1. In what areas of my job am I or was I an innovator?
2. In what areas of my job am I or was I an early adopter?
3. In what areas of my job am I or was I in the early majority?
4. In what areas of my job am I or was I in the late majority?
5. In what areas of my job am I or was I a laggard?

Before asking these questions, it is useful to identify and define the specific domains that need to be considered; for preference, these should be domains that will be strategically important during the forthcoming 36 to 60 months.

> STEP 4: PAIR-IT

After a brief period of thought, invite the participants to walk through the different stages of the curve in pairs, in an order that they themselves are free to choose. They must, however, walk through all the different stages and in each stage must share their individual answers to the question relevant to that stage.

> STEP 5: REFLECT-ON-IT

After all the pairs have walked through the curve, bring the group back together, so that they can share their insights and experiences. Focus in particular on the strengths that came to light for each stage.

> STEP 6: QUESTION-IT

Encourage the participants to reflect more deeply. Let them choose one of the following questions to answer:

1. Where do I position myself in the innovation curve in my personal life?
2. Where do I position myself in the innovation curve in my professional life?
3. Where, in my opinion, is our company positioned in the innovation curve?
4. Where, in my opinion, do others position our company in the innovation curve?
5. Where, in my opinion, should our company ideally be positioned in the innovation curve?
6. If I were to start up my own company, where ideally would I want it to be positioned in the innovation curve?

The effect can be stronger if the participants are asked while answering to stand in the stage of the curve to which their question refers. Invite the participants to elaborate further on their answers.

Exercise 3: Future mapping

This exercise was initially devised by Mikael Ahlström, although at the time when he first developed it no one gave a second thought to either pandemics or Zoonotics. The basic idea is to sketch a shared picture of important trends in the past, the present and the future of a particular branch or sector. It is useful to look not only at the trends in your own branch or sector, but also (in fact, above all) in other branches and sectors. Simply focusing on your own branch or sector in the hope of becoming a Zoonotic is a complete waste of time.

Ask the participants to list briefly the trends of last year, this year and the next 36 months. Having done this, ask them to try to identify any patterns that may emerge and also to assess the extent to which the trends are relevant for your company. Focus in particular on impactful trends that have a significant effect on society, culture, diversity, inclusion, technology, activism, etc. If you think it more appropriate in your circumstances, you can focus on just a single specific trend; for example, the reduction of harmful impact on the climate.

It can often get quite noisy during this workshop, so there is a risk that the more timid participants are not heard. Make sure that everyone is given the chance to have their say.

> STEP 1: TAPE-IT
Either use a large wall that you can divide into three with tape or else three large and separate flip charts or tables without chairs. Mark the three sections as follows: this year +1; this year +2; this year +3.

> STEP 2 POST-IT & PACE-IT
Give each participant a pen and some post-it notes. Position them in a semi-circle in front of the wall, flip charts or tables. Explain the purpose of the workshop and give them the following instructions:
1. As a group, we are going to create a vision for the future by looking through the lenses of the past and the present.

2. Each participant is free to add post-its to the three time frames of the exercise. Each post-it should be marked with one significant strength (trend, technology, political movement, behavioural change, etc.).
3. Each participant must read out loud what is written on the post-it before sticking it on the appropriate time frame.
4. It is not necessary to wait your turn. As soon as you have written something on a post-it, you can stick it in position.
5. Don't think too long. The idea is that within a quarter of an hour the space for each of the three time frames is full.
6. This time pressure is an essential part of the process; it encourages spontaneity and avoids too much soul-searching.

Start with the next year. Give the participants three minutes to stick their post-its in position. Then do the same with the following year and the year after that. Encourage the participants to work quickly and not to hesitate too much. Don't be afraid to challenge them with questions or suggestions.

> STEP 3: PATTERN-IT

Once the quarter of an hour is finished, ask the group to return to the semi-circle. Invite them to look at all the post-its in each of the three sections and to search for possible patterns. Once a pattern has been found, it can be marked out by adding a coloured sticker to the relevant post-its. If there is enough time, ask them to make a summary of the patterns that have been discovered for each of the three years.

> STEP 4: RUN-IT

Now ask the participants to think and discuss as a group the results that have so far emerged. You can stimulate their discussion with the following questions:
1. What patterns have become visible?
2. Which patterns are important for you as individual participants and for the company as a whole, so that we need to know more about them?
3. What are your thoughts and feelings about the past, the present and the future?
4. What are the consequences for you, our team, our company and our sector?

> STEP 5: WRAP-IT

Wind up the session with a summary of the core themes that emerged during the discussions. Ask the group what ideas and actions are now important for the future. Ask each participant to name one idea or action point that he/she will take away from this exercise. Zoonotic leaders will have a tendency to start work immediately on the best ideas. Perhaps in this way you will be able to discover who are the natural leaders in your team, but who have remained hidden until now.

Exercise 4: Zoonotic builder

To develop Zoonotic concepts requires a method that encourages the participants to generate ideas in brainstorming sessions as a team; ideas that combine different Unfair Advantages with a viral power.

This method starts with a brainstorm on a number of broad themes, such as sustainability, inclusion, activism and other matters that we have under our control and can provide us with an Unfair Advantage. It is also possible to start in a more focused manner by working on more specific themes, such as climate change, income inequality and obesity, if these themes offer possibilities for gaining a strategic advantage. Remember, however, that with this kind of more focused approach there is a risk that you will overlook a number of other potentially disruptive Zoonotic strategies.

The purpose of the brainstorm is to combine ideas from different sectors, along the lines that we discussed in chapter 1 of part 1: Bird = Unfair Advantage 1, Bat = Unfair Advantage 2, Pig = the new combination or Superspreader, and the Zoonotic is the resultant product.

At the end of the session, choose the ideas that seem to have the most potential to become the strongest Zoonotics.

The participants should be asked to stand during the session and make use of stirring music in the background to keep things moving along at pace. People's reactions need to be spontaneous. To add an element of time pressure, call out regularly how much time is still left (set a clear limit). My inspiration for this approach comes in part from the many workshops of this kind I have led over the years and in part from the Hyper Island and IDEO Ideation methods.

> STEP 1: FRAME-IT

Focus primarily on trends that have the potential to be possible game-changers but are not yet prominently visible on most people's radar. For example, you can concentrate on:
- Unfair technologies: smartphones, 3D printing, GPS;
- Unfair human needs: love, waking up in the morning;
- Unfair services: Google Translate, Spotify, Candy Crush.

A successful session starts by outlining a well-defined opportunity, resulting from the following open, optimistic, solution-oriented question: 'How could we...?' This question must be sufficiently broad in nature, but must also take a concrete situation as its starting point. An example: in a session intended to improve patient experience in a hospital, the starter question was: 'How could we better support the families of patients in the hospital?'

If the 'How could we...?' question results in the description of an Unfair Advantage, different teams then need to think about possible ideas to further exploit this advantage. It is important that they continually put forward unexpected and unusual suggestions, which can perhaps be combined to make brilliant new ideas.

Divide the participants into three groups, each standing around a table. Give them roughly three minutes to brainstorm each idea. If an idea or a concept for an Unfair Advantage emerges, note it down on a post-it note and stick it on the table. At the end of the brainstorming, there should be a number of different ideas on each table.

> STEP 2: GENERATE-IT

Using the ideas on the table, give the participants twelve minutes to come up with as many Zoonotic ideas as they can. A Zoonotic idea is a combination of two or more Unfair Advantages to create a totally new concept with exponential growth potential.

Summarise each Zoonotic idea on a sheet of A4 paper. Describe the ideas that have been combined and give the result a catchy name. For example: Mopit = home cleaning + ApplePay + iPad. Keep the tempo high, to avoid boredom setting in. The aim is to find as many possible combinations as you can, because this will increase the chances of one of them being a truly brilliant Zoonotic.

> STEP 3: NARROW-IT

When the time allowed for the brainstorm has elapsed, collect together all the results and stick them on the wall. Ask each group to present its own Zoonotic ideas to the other two groups. Invite all three groups to evaluate the potential Zoonotic power of each of the different concepts.

In the final phase, each group chooses its own favourite concept and is given half an hour to work out the details for the refinement of the functionalities of the business model that will allow the concept to be put into practice. Once again, each detailed plan is put to the other two groups for comment and assessment.

> STEP 4: SPREAD-IT

Use worksheets based on the example below to structure all three concepts. Put all the various Unfair Advantages on both sides and the Superspreader in the middle. Combine items from both lists to create as many products, services or experiences as possible.

To be clear: choose two broad categories that have no connection with each other; for example, hospitals and hotels. Think beyond your own branch or sector. Then add your Superspreader to the combined Unfair Advantages.

During the debriefing, ask the participants to reflect on the following questions:
1. What did it feel like to work in this kind of creative manner?
2. Was it easy? Difficult? Challenging?
3. What was your reaction? How did you behave?
4. What insights has this exercise given you about yourself?
5. What insights has this exercise given you about the development of new ideas?
6. How can you apply these insights in the future?

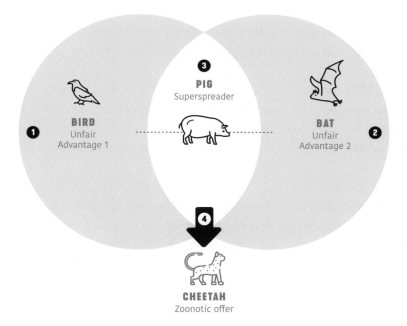

BIRD
Unfair
Advantage 1

PIG
Superspreader

BAT
Unfair
Advantage 2

CHEETAH
Zoonotic offer

Exercise 5: Strategic planning

This is a reflection exercise on a limited scale that is intended to encourage the participants to react appropriately to a Zoonotic attack. It is an exercise that complements exercise 4 above. The participants first reach agreement about a Zoonotic vision and then sketch out the necessary steps to bring it about.

⯈ STEP 1: ENVISION-IT

Explain that the intention is to draw up a concrete plan to protect your company against the impact of a Zoonotic.

Take as your starting point the assumption that six months have passed and that you have achieved your own Zoonotic objective and are now looking back at everything you did during that period to make it possible.

Let the participants start with the Zoonotic concepts from exercise 4. Split them up into three groups. Each group starts by discussing the Zoonotic vision of each participant, with the aim of quickly reaching a common vision. This vision is then expressed on a large sheet of paper, using as many images and as few words as possible and only covering the right side of the sheet of paper.

> STEP 2: HELP-IT

After consultation within the groups, write at the top of the sheet at least five factors that could help to realise the Zoonotic vision. These factors can relate to matters such as culture, people, opportunities, technologies, situations, etc.

> STEP 3: SUPPORT-IT

Again after consultation, write at the bottom of the sheet at least five factors that could support the realisation of the Zoonotic vision. Again, these factors can relate to matters such as culture, people, opportunities, technologies, situations, etc.

> STEP 4: ACTION-IT

The participants must now add in on the left-hand side of the sheet the actions that must be taken to realise the Zoonotic vision. This left-hand side should be divided into three sections, in which the concrete steps should be written down and clearly explained. This is no longer a matter of concepts, but a one-page summary of the details that are necessary to take the first steps towards the realisation of the vision.

> STEP 5: CLOSE-IT

The three groups share their visions and action plans with each other. Finish by asking each participant what they will do differently in their job from now on.

Exercise 6: Tracing undesirable consequences

The purpose of this exercise is to search for possible undesirable consequences resulting from a Zoonotic strategy that makes use of new technologies, with the aim of making improvements where necessary, so that you can avoid becoming a Predatory Zoonotic. The participants are challenged to look beyond what is generally known about a particular technology, in order to identify possibly damaging effects that may become evident in the long term. Each team must try to think of as many negative effects as it possibly can. These effects are then assessed by one of the other teams.

> STEP 1: SHOCK-IT

Divide the participants into three groups of three to five people. Start the exercise by telling the cautionary story of Robinhood: how their platform was originally intended as a low-cost, low-threshold manner to conduct stock market transactions, but after an initial period of success degenerated, thanks to the greed of the developers, into an addictive and casino-like game of chance, as a result of which many clients lost large sums of money, leading in one case to the suicide of a man who suddenly discovered that he was in debt to the tune of 730,000 dollars. It was only after this incident that the developers belatedly amended their platform with regard to the manner in which stock options were traded. Explain to the participants that their task in this workshop is to trace as many possible undesired effects in certain technology situations as they can, so that they can then develop the best possible Zoonotic ideas by avoiding them.

> STEP 2: LIST-IT

Give each group five minutes to fill in five post-its with at least five new technologies or new business applications. For example: vaccines, Netflix, Instagram, Google Maps, etc. Challenge the participants to include in particular technologies that are popular outside their own age group.

> STEP 3: BINGE-IT

Via a brainstorming, ask each group to suggest at least three undesirable consequences for each of the five post-its. For Netflix, for example, this might be: the addictive effect of binge-watching, a lack of physical movement (exercise), or a lack of sleep. Encourage the participants to give their imagination free rein. In this exercise, there is no such thing as a 'wrong' answer.

Note down each idea on a separate post-it. After five or so minutes, ask the groups to share their ideas with each other.

> STEP 4: FIX-IT

Now invite the participants to think of a possible solution for each undesired effect. For example: make Netflix free of charge if you only watch one episode at a time or make users pay extra if they are guilty of binge-watching.

Once again, encourage them to let their fantasy run wild. What if their new idea is worse than the original? No problem! You can never know whether or not in the future a competitor might emerge for whom this idea is a valuable one.

After seven minutes, ask the groups to share their ideas with each other. When they have done so, give them another seven minutes to develop new solutions on the basis of what they have just heard.

> STEP 5: REFLECT-IT

To finish off, allow the participants to reflect on the most unexpected and the most valuable ideas to emerge from the session. You can also ask them to share the most important insights that they have gained from this exercise.

Exercise 7: Point of departure

This exercise is intended to help a new team to determine the direction, structure and first steps that can lead towards the development of the Zoonotic project. The participants are asked to process a number of documents and answer a number of questions, which they then share with each other in a digital format. You can either use dynamic documents that evolve further as the project progresses, or else compact summaries that serve as an appropriate starting point. My inspiration for this exercise comes from Johanna Olsson, but I have adjusted it to suit our Zoonotic purposes.

> STEP 1: EXPLAIN-IT

Gather the participants together and do a brief check-in, to make sure that everyone is 100 percent physically and mentally focused. Explain that this is a short workshop, the purpose of which is to give a clear direction and structure to the future Zoonotic project. The emphasis is on speed and focus. The group is then asked to answer eight questions. They must first note down their answers on paper and then transfer them to a digital document that can be shared. To keep the exercise as dynamic as possible, it is a good idea to have the participants standing at a table, flip chart or whiteboard.

> STEP 2: FOCUS-IT

To encourage Cheetah-like speed, make a 'parking space' on the wall where topics or questions can be 'parked' that do not immediately help to answer the main questions quickly. Agree that you will only return to the contents of this parking space later on.

> STEP 3: TIME-IT

Also agree clearly in advance how much time will be allowed and divide this equally between the eight questions. If you allow an hour and a half, this means roughly eleven minutes for each question. Your role as facilitator is to keep an eye on the time and to ensure that everyone remains properly focused.

> STEP 4: QUESTION-IT

Hang up a poster that you have prepared beforehand with the following questions. Ask the participants to deal with them one by one within the allotted time.

1. Goal
    a. What is the general goal of the Zoonotic project?
    b. Summarise this in a single sentence.
2. Desired result
    a. What concrete results do we wish to achieve with this project?
    b. Outline these results in two to four bullet points.

3. Target group and value

    a. For whom is this project intended?

    b. What value are we offering them?

    c. Summarise in three bullet points or less.

4. Roles

Who is involved in the project and what are their responsibilities? Here are some suggestions for possible roles:

- Leader: the owner of the project.
- Wingman: the most important support for the leader on a daily basis.
- Core: the group of key personnel who work together on the project.
- Adviser: people who the members of the core team can turn to for input and feedback.
- Decision-makers: people who have the authority to give final approval to the project.

5. Milestones and budget

    a. What needs to happen and when?

    b. What budget is available?

    c. Summarise in bullet points.

6. How?

    a. How will the team collaborate?

    b. How will communication take place, tasks be divided, decisions be taken?

    c. Write five key guidelines, each with a short description.

7. Success and fiasco criteria

    a. What does success look like for this Zoonotic?

    b. What does failure look like for this Zoonotic?

    c. Describe each scenario in four or five bullet points.

8. Connections

    a. Which other projects have a possible connection with the Zoonotic project?

    b. Are there other documents and sources that need to be considered?

    c. Make a list of the most crucial documents or sources.

> STEP 5: WRAP-IT

Agree who will gather together all the collected answers in a digital document to be shared with the team. Before ending the session, give the project leadership the opportunity to clarify any possible questions that still remain outstanding.

> STEP 6: ACTION-IT

Finish with a check-out in which each participant states what his/her next action point will be in relation to the project. The check-in and the check-out are both intended to convince the participants of the importance of everyone's individual and collective engagement, if the project is to be a success. The check-in emphasises the need for commitment, focus and effort. The check-out emphasises the need for reflection and completion.

Tip: If it is not possible to retain all of the suggested projects, the wrap-up session is above all intended to allow people to learn from the experience, provide support for each other and part from each other in a manner that encourages continued connectedness. This is possible through the sharing of personal high points and low points, which can lead on to discussions about personal learning points. Everyone should be asked to describe a number of concrete actions that he/she will take away from the exercise and will use in future projects. In addition, all the participants will be expected to give feedback and will receive it in return, which will allow all concerned to grow further.

INSIGHT

› Are you fully up to speed in TikTok land?

New media bring with them new rules of the game, which you need to learn as quickly as possible if you don't want to be branded as old-fashioned and out of date. For example, it is useful to know that TikTok ranks content on the basis of a number of factors, starting (naturally enough) with the things that you say interest you as a new user, but also taking account of things that might not interest you at all. The other factors that play a role are:

1. User interactions: for example, the videos that you 'like', the accounts that you follow, the comments that you post and the content that you create.
2. Video information: details such as captions, sounds and hashtags.
3. Device and account settings: your language preference, your country and your type of device.

Each of these factors is included and weighted in TikTok's For You recommendation system, as a result of which each For You page (#fy) is unique and completely attuned to the interests of the user. These interests can be deduced, for example, by the fact that you are prepared to watch a fairly long video right through to the end. This factor is then given more weight by the algorithm than the fact, say, that the viewer and the creator both live in the same country.

So does this means you need to have thousands of followers if you want to go viral? TikTok's answer is short and unequivocal: no. Although a video made by someone with more followers has more chance of being seen, neither the number of followers nor the number of views attracted by previous videos count as factors in the recommendation system.

Even so, I continue to have a problem with the fact that using TikTok still involves a security risk. Do we really need to give the Chinese such easy access to our data and our markets, when we find it so difficult to get similar access to theirs?

MOVEMBER ENABLES MEN TO DISCUSS CANCER

The Movember Foundation makes people aware of different types of cancer, such as prostate cancer, which often occur in men. The Movember Foundation has developed into a viral sensation.

1. What is the creative idea and who benefits from it?

The idea was the brainchild of two friends sitting in a bar in Australia. The intention was to make cancer and particularly male cancer discussable, so that the early tracing and diagnosis of the disease could be improved, which would eventually save many lives. Right at the very beginning, the initial plan was for men to start the month of November with a clean-shaven face, but then to let their moustache grow for the rest of the month and take photographs of it, which could be posted online. As with the Ice Bucket Challenge, this made it possible for the participants to pass on the message easily and with a distinctive personal touch. As time has passed, so the campaign has evolved. There was a Father & Sons edition, in which dads shared their moustache wisdom with their offspring, and there has also been a Generation Mo edition, which aimed to attract a younger public. The foundation also organises events, such as Move in Movember, which encourages people to take more exercise. Over the years, Movember has developed into a real community. In 2013, it doubled its Facebook reach and retweets on Twitter grew by 45 percent. In 2014, Movember collected 1.2 million mentions on social media. The hashtag #Movember became the new online hit and the helpline of Prostate Cancer UK also began to receive significantly more calls. In that same year, 21 countries took part in the campaign, all with their own local website and donation programme.

UNDER THE MICROSCOPE

2. What stimulates people to share the idea?

People find it amusing to change their appearance by growing a moustache or a beard and then sharing photos of their 'new look' with their family, friends and colleagues.

3. How can you use time pressure to speed up the process?

In theory, the action is limited to the month of November each year, although in practice it tends to also cover the preceding and following months.

4. How do you get the support of big names?

Numerous celebrities were willing to take part, including Justin Bieber, Mel Gibson, Clive Owen, Kellan Lutz and Sylvester Stallone.

5. How can you use short and memorable videos?

The real strength of this challenge is that it can easily be adapted to suit the individual. It offers an opportunity to give your support a personal touch, as well as allowing the more adventurous souls to show their creativity. Both these factors are important if you want to develop a viral business strategy: how can you let people display their individuality and their inventiveness? Also make sure that the hashtags get noticed and are rewarded. Of course, it has also got to be fun. With Movember, sharing a photo of the result is just one small part of that fun. The campaign has grown to become a shining example for all social media managers and is unquestionably a viral sensation.

6. How does your campaign motivate altruism?

Some people take part just for the fun of it, but for many it is an open invitation to talk about often sensitive health issues.

7. How do you ensure that the threshold to participate is as low as possible?

> With Movember, you are free to choose how you want to participate: you
> can just let your moustache grow or, alternatively, agree to run a total
> of 60 miles in the course of the month November. Sixty symbolises the
> number of people who commit suicide somewhere in the world each
> hour. Thanks to the Movember mobile app, it is very easy to donate
> money to one of their good causes, as well as to post your photos online.

Although the use of the word 'cancer' appears nowhere in this campaign, I still regard it as a highly successful viral action. In a very low-threshold way it reaches a broad group of people in a playful manner that encourages them to reflect on serious health problems. Moreover, fundraising is not immediately central, which underlines that this is not a begging-bowl action, but an awareness campaign.

chECKLIst

START YOUR VIRAL BUSINESS STRATEGY FROM YOUR CORE: YOUR UNFAIR ADVANTAGE.

SEARCH FOR ANOTHER UNFAIR ADVANTAGE THAT YOU CAN COMBINE WITH YOUR OWN TO CREATE A NEW PRODUCT OR SERVICE.

LET THE ZOONOTIC LEADER LEAD THE DANCE. HE/SHE:

- IS A CREATIVE HACKER.
- IS PERFORMANCE-DRIVEN.
- COMBINES IQ WITH EQ.
- BELIEVES IN STAKEHOLDER CAPITALISM.
- SEARCHES FOR LATENT NEEDS.
- USES MACHINE LEARNING.
- SEES EVERYTHING IN SHARPER FOCUS.

AN AGILE ZOONOTIC TEAM IS A MUST:

- GIVE THE YOUNG CUBS A CHANCE.
- EVERYTHING DEPENDS ON MUTUAL TRUST.
- BIG HAIRY AUDACIOUS GOALS ARE THE BINDER.
- LOOK BEYOND THE BOUNDARIES OF YOUR OWN SECTOR/COUNTRY.

DEVELOP YOUR OWN ZOONOTIC STRATEGY VIA CREATIVE WORKSHOPS:

- GET STARTED BY USING THE EXERCISES IN PART 2.

PART 3

HOW CAN YOU FIGHT A ZOONOTIC?

If you find yourself threatened by a Zoonotic, you only have a limited number of options to defend yourself. It is almost certain that the Zoonotic will continue to grow and get stronger, but the end result is very difficult to predict, because you do not know when the Zoonotic is likely to reach its peak. One thing is certain: the likelihood that you will be able to return to 'business as usual' in the near future is almost non-existent. For this reason, it is equally certain that you need to prepare yourself in the best possible way to counteract the possible arrival of a Zoonotic in your sector. If you fail to do so, the consequences can often be disastrous, not only for you and your company, but also for your staff and your suppliers.

If you want to implement an effective policy in time of crisis, this means that you first need to put your finances in order during the good times, so that you can build up a buffer of the resources that will help you to fight back. (Think, for example, of the shortage of face masks at the start of the corona crisis.) Once the crisis hits, it will be too late to react. You need to have your defences ready in advance, prepared at a moment when your head was cool and the pressure was off. Do not make the crucial mistake of thinking that it can never happen to you. There are a growing number of Zoonotics everywhere, and one is probably coming your way.

In our hyper-connected digital world, you have a choice, just like the Cheetah on the savannah: you can hunt or be hunted. I assume that you prefer the first of these two options. But this means that you must be prepared to fight and it is vital that you begin those preparations now! You must start taking the measures that will allow you to become your own Zoonotic or at the very least will allow you to identify the advent of a hostile Zoonotic in your industry at the earliest possible moment.

"
Trying to copy a Zoonotic is a worthless form of defence.
"

You cannot stop a Zoonotic simply by copying it,
no matter how hard you try. You need to develop your own
Zoonotic defence strategy appropriate to your company.
Speed is the key to success.

Whereas part 2 focused on what is necessary to develop an offensive Zoonotic strategy, part 3 will concentrate on the requirements for an effective defensive strategy. The nature of your approach will depend on the speed and the extent to which you recognise the seriousness and the scale of the Zoonotic threat.

1

DEVELOP AN INFLUENCER STRATEGY NOW

If you do not yet have an influencer strategy, it is high time that you started one NOW. If you wait until the Zoonotic strikes, you will already be too late. Trying to develop an influencer network in the middle of a crisis is like trying to make friends who can help you to move house on the day of your removals. It just does not work. If you want to know in depth how to develop an effective influencer strategy, I recommend you take a look at my first book: *Influencers*. Who are they? Where do you find them? And how do they light the fire? I will confine myself here to a summary of the main points.

Why influencer marketing?

During a study trip to San Francisco, I spoke with Wilson White, who is a fascinating man, not least because of the unusual combination of his university diplomas: he is both an engineer and a jurist. He told me that at one point Google was worried about the quality of advertising, in part because 615 million computers and other devices are still fitted with an ad blocker. It is not that people hate advertising per se, but they do dislike receiving advertising that is not relevant to them. For this reason Google decided to launch the Coalition for Better Ads. This service gives consumers the opportunity to mute advertisements that do not appeal to them. In 2017 alone, this prompted more than 5 million reactions, so that it was possible to prevent 40 million advertising messages from being sent to places where they were not wanted.

It is clear that traditional advertising is systematically losing its grip on consumers. Its place is being taken by influencer marketing. Using influencers allows brands to land exactly where they want to be: at the heart of purchasing decisions. Influencers develop authentic person-to-person relationships with consumers. In other words, influencers not only take over part of the role of mass communication, but are also better in that role. Because even in the golden years of traditional advertising consumers never had as much trust in brands as they do in influencers today.

It is precisely because of this relationship of trust that an influencer can be of huge value during a Zoonotic crisis. Why? Because an influencer's public loves to listen to what he/she has to say and attaches great importance to his/her opinions and recommendations. With the right influencer policy, you can convert trust in the influencer into trust in your product. This will give you a vital lead over your competitors that will very quickly become an unbridgeable gap. Because a good influencer knows what works in his network and when.

What's more, one influencer can often bring you into contact with others. If you can convince the five to ten of the most influential voices in your sector to come on board, you can cut the influencing legs out from under your rivals, leaving them isolated and vulnerable.

In other words, there are at least two very good reasons for starting an influencer strategy NOW. In addition, a good influencer network can also serve as a kind of early warning system, which can make you aware of the possible awakening of a slumbering Zoonotic. And once the Zoonotic is fully on the prowl, influencers can further help you to fend off its attacks or at least weaken them.

What is influencer marketing?

It is always useful to have a clear definition that gets to the heart of the matter. So here it is:

> 'Influencer marketing is an action plan that strengthens your consumer-to-consumer marketing messages through people who communicate with them in such a contextually relevant and meaningful way that they succeed in persuading others to take action.'

Influencer marketing is a form of innovative marketing. In the modern business world, it is a new added value in your media mix. But this does not mean that it is now the only communication channel on which you should focus. The biggest return is best obtained through a combination of channels. In other words, influencer marketing should be added to your existing mix of traditional and other new media. Or better still, try to achieve cross-fertilisation between your different channels.

What does influencer marketing look like?

On the basis of the above definition, it is possible to identify the four key characteristics of an influencer.

AN INFLUENCER IS…

A PERSON	WHO SPREADS CONTEXTU-ALLY RELEVANT MESSAGES	WHICH ARE SO MEANINGFUL	THAT THEY PERSUADE OTHERS TO TAKE ACTION
An influencer is not an organisation or a PR team. Nor is he/she necessarily an ambassador for your brand.	By working together with influencers, as a brand you reach the right people in the right way at the right moment.	Influencers are very close to their networks. As a result, they help you to produce content that is perfectly attuned to the needs and expectations of their community (= your consumers). In this way, you build up credibility.	Impact on behaviour is crucial. It is this that makes influencers so valuable for companies. In a dream scenario, influencer content (for example, a product review) is the decisive factor in the consumer's purchasing decision.

There is even a formula to estimate the value of an influencer:

Influence = reach x engagement x relevance

1. Reach

Reach is the influencer's total number of followers. The bigger his/her public, the more people you can potentially reach.

2. Engagement

The reach of an influencer says nothing about his/her relationship with his/her network. The more interactions (likes, shares, reactions) an influencer can generate, the stronger the connection with his/her followers will be.

3. Relevance

Have you found someone with thousands of followers and a constant stream of interactions? Good: this person does indeed have influencer potential. But his/her value for your brand, product or service may be zero. The success of influencer marketing is dependent on the extent of the match between your company and the influencer. Society figure Astrid Bryan is, for example, a relevant choice for a brand like GingerLove. Her network consists of people who are likely to welcome content about hip ginger tea and share it with others. But it would not be such a good idea for Elon Musk to use her to try to sell Teslas. In that case, messages about high-tech cars would probably not be so interesting for Astrid's fans. Finding a good match between influencer and company is more than a question of gut feeling. It is something you need to calculate on the basis of the behaviour of the influencer's followers.

It is by using this combination of reach, engagement and relevance that you will be able to identify the most valuable influencers in your sector. But that is by no means the end of the matter. You will want your influencers to offer their followers different content at different times. To allow this to happen as efficiently as possible, this means that you will have to segment your various influencers.

The creators of the influencer marketing tool Traackr distinguish between ten different influencer personas. These are an excellent aid for your segmentation process.

- **The CELEBRITY >** Pascale Naessens (bestselling author of cookbooks)
  'My public is larger than the population of Ghent or Utrecht.'
- **The AUTHORITY >** Marion Debruyne (dean of the Vlerick Business School)
  'My opinion is worth its weight in gold in my field of expertise.'
- **The CONNECTOR >** Elke Jeurissen (founder of Glassroots and Straffe Madammen) *'I like bringing together different pieces of the puzzle.'*
- **The PERSONAL BRAND >** Linda De Mol (actress and TV host)
  'My name is my biggest capital.'
- **The ANALYST >** Imke Courtois (football international and analyst for Sporza TV)
  'I create and spread valuable insights.'
- **The ACTIVIST >** Michel Vandenbosch (chairman of animal welfare organisation GAIA) *'My faith can move mountains.'*
- **The EXPERT >** Carole Lamarque (founding partner Duval Union Consulting)
  'I have written books about my work.'
- **The INSIDER >** Michel Maus (professor and columnist)
  'I am a respected source with my own agenda.'
- **The INNOVATOR >** Rudi Pauwels (founder of Biocartis)
  'I question things and stimulate debate.'
- **The JOURNALIST >** Wim De Preter (business journalist for *De Tijd*)
  'I am the face of the new news industry.'

Of course, if your company or organisation is unique, your influencer segments will need to reflect this as well. The above roles are not engraved in tablets of stone; they are moulded in clay. Shape them gently until they become the segments that match your company. For example, your sector might be devoid of activists, but there may be another group that has a loud voice that people wish to listen to.

Have you already determined the segmentation that is best for you? That is certainly a good start, but, once again, it is not the end of the matter. You need to re-examine your segments each time you start a new campaign or action. Is the existing classification ideal for helping you to meet the objectives of your latest plan? The answer to this question is often 'no'. As a result, it is sometimes worth splitting up segments into sub-segments.

From storytelling to storydoing

Influencers love stories. Do you know the most important ambitions of your organisation? Good. Then you also know the direction your storytelling should take. In your story, you translate your positioning as a brand into added value for your customers. Why do you do what you do? And how do you do it? The messages spread by your influencers must connect with your core story.

However, you can get even more out of your influencers by 'storydoing'. This means that your entire organisation acts in function of your story. Storytelling is often directed by your internal marketing and communication department or by an external bureau. But with storydoing, your story is actually embedded in the DNA of all your employees. It is the ultimate proof that your story is authentic. Storydoing of this kind is a highly fruitful way to collaborate with influencers. You immediately start with a bonus:

- Your organisation and your communication already have a heart, a soul and credibility.
- Your staff offer influencers plenty of inspiration for authentic and original content.
- Your target group is already engaged with the story.

The following six questions will allow you to discover to what extent you are currently engaged in storytelling and storydoing. If you answer 'yes' to the first three questions, storytelling already has a place in your company. The following three questions determine how far you have progressed with storydoing.

1. Do you have a story?
2. Does everyone in your organisation understand and value the story?
3. Does the story direct the decisions, actions and behaviour of your organisation?
4. Does your story contain an ambition that goes beyond a purely commercial goal?
5. Do you take bold and iconic decisions that reflect your story?
6. Do people outside your company talk about your story?

IKEA is an excellent example of a storydoing company. Their story is anchored in their mission: 'To create a better everyday life for many people'. This mission results in the setting of a number of goals that are clearly not commercial, such as investment in sustainability. This objective has an impact on the company's decisions, which is something they like to communicate:

'IKEA wants to have a positive impact on the planet. For this reason, we are fully committed to the things that are truly important: we are converting all our lighting to energy-efficient LEDs and all the cotton for our products comes from sustainable sources.'

The IKEA story is known and valued outside the company. In 2016, Universum conducted a survey among 700,000 students and recent graduates about the attractiveness of a number of well-known employers. In Sweden, IKEA was shown to be the country's most highly regarded organisation in this respect.

No goals, no glory

Have you already clearly established the positioning and story of your company? You have? Great! In that case, dealing with the strategic and operational aspects of your influencer marketing should be a piece of cake! Let's start with the objectives of your influencer marketing. These will sound familiar to every marketeer. The channels may change over time, but the most important marketing objectives always remain the same.

1. **Awareness:** use your influencers to attract attention for your company with a new public, to improve your brand image or to boost the name recognition of a newly launched product.

2. **Sales:** use your influencer marketing campaign to generate more leads and sales; a positive contact with an influencer will bring your potential customers a step further into your sales funnel.

3. Retention: use your influencers to stimulate the loyalty of your existing customers and to boost your Net Promoter Score (NPS). In crisis situations, the right influencers are of incalculable value to limit damage to your image.

When should you use influencers?

The objectives listed above need to be carefully coordinated with the timing of your influencer marketing. Influencers can be employed in every phase of the life cycle of your product, service or event. Think, for example, of influencers who use social media to let people know that they will be present at your congress. This will convince some of the influencer's followers that the congress is worth attending, so that they will buy a ticket.

Another application? Use the feedback of your influencers as input for your product development. Often, they are so-called 'power users', who use your product intensively and are familiar with all its functions. Moreover, their content (for example, a video review or a request for an extra feature on Twitter) is just the tip of the iceberg. In the reactions to their content, you can immediately see how much support a complaint, compliment or request gets from their network.

In summary: decide what (product, process or customer-oriented) you want to communicate, for what purpose (awareness, sale or retention) and at what moment (product launch, lead generation campaign, crisis), so that you can make best use of your influencers to achieve your goals. The result of this exercise is a short vision text that will be the foundation of your influencer marketing. This vision will be attuned to your wider business strategy and everyone in your organisation will know what function your influencer marketing fulfils. It is on the basis of this vision that you must choose your influencers and types of content.

Five ways to find influencers

You now know the direction you want to travel with your influencer marketing. The next challenge is to actually find the influencers who are best able to help you achieve your marketing objectives.

Here are five possible places where you can go fishing for them. Let's hope you hook one!

1. Search engines

You had better roll up your sleeves, because this kind of work takes a lot of time and effort. No less than 84 percent of all searches for influencers are manual! To start, you need to collect together a number of relevant terms about your sector, company, product, service or event. Type them into a search engine and see what happens. Google is, of course, the most well known. For further investigation, limit yourself to just the first page of search results. If a possibly interesting blogger immediately appears, you can be confident that he/she is already familiar with search engine optimisation (SEO). This is an added bonus, because it means that via this blogger you can also reach other people who type in relevant keywords.

Most social networks are also search engines. Repeat the same exercise on websites like Twitter and YouTube. The results will usually be ordered on the basis of reach or engagement, two key parameters from the influence formula. On YouTube you can also sort on the basis of the number of times a video has been viewed. Twitter similarly shows you top tweets that get the biggest number of likes, reactions and retweets.

2. Software tools

Software tools can likewise help you to find, filter and sort influencers. For example, you can rank all the users of a social network on the basis of authority in a particular subject, location or other useful parameters. With Engagor you can monitor all social media updates that appear about your company, as well as finding out which messages are most frequently shared. The software of Traackr makes it possible for you to segment and analyse influencers.

3. Marketplaces

A marketplace is a site that brings brands and influencers into contact with each other. A brand is often able to search through a databank of influencers with the particular needs of a planned campaign in mind. As an added advantage, the influencers are also already interested in working with you. In The Netherlands and Belgium, Influo has built such a marketplace. Also in The Netherlands, The Cirqle likewise facilitates collaboration between brands and influencers.

4. Events

A fourth good way to search for and approach influencers? Events. In particular, keep your eyes open at sector events. The speakers will often be influencers. Also type the hashtag of your event in your smartphone and take a look at the most active twitterers, because not every influencer likes speaking in public. In fact, there are many influencers who feel more comfortable in their familiar internet biotope.

In addition to sectoral events, more and more other events are now being organised in which the role of influencers is central. This is especially the case with YouTube influencers. Because they work with images and sound, they develop a very strong bond with their fans. As a result, they often grow into mini-celebrities, who are very well known in their medium.

5. Influencer bureaus

Finally, brands on the lookout for influencers can also use specialised bureaus. This limits your time investment to a minimum. Influencer bureaus have their own networks of influencers who operate in many different fields. Most bureaus further offer a wide range of services for each phase of your influencer marketing strategy. This starts with the selection of the most suitable influencers, following which they often take over the management of the project and the further communication with the influencers. Some also play a role in the production of influencer content. Others have tools that collect and clearly visualise your campaign data. Examples of this kind of bureau in the Low Countries include The Kube (Antwerp) and IMA (Amsterdam).

Influencer found. What now?

Have you identified suitable influencers in your market? Follow them all on social media, even the ones who you probably won't work with. By following influencers in this way, you kill two birds with one stone:

1. It gives you your first positive contact with the influencers. They invest a lot of
   time and energy in extending their reach and are always happy whenever they
   get an extra follower. At the same time, you let the influencer know that he/she
   has appeared on your radar.
2. It means that you are always up to date. You can read about all the newest
   trends in your field and are kept abreast of all the latest news. You can even see
   which of your competitors are most frequently mentioned by the influencers.

Influencer marketing is a business collaboration between a brand and an influencer. In other words, it is a two-way street that works both ways. Influencers also
have a strategy they wish to follow and objectives they want to realise. For example, they may want to provide their network with content that has added value.

You need to be aware of these things. Ask your influencer partner about his/her
expectation for your collaboration. In this way, you will learn more about his/her
main objectives and also be able to assess how far you might be able to help him/
her achieve them. Traackr has details for each of its basic segments about what
you as a company can offer each type of influencer.

- **The CELEBRITY > offer sponsoring possibilities.**
  Sometimes you might get lucky, if the celebrity is already a big fan of your
  product. But in most cases you buy his/her attention. Sponsor agreements
  can meet the wishes of both parties.
- **The AUTHORITY > offer added value for his/her community.**
  You can't buy an authority; you have to convince them. For example, with
  high-quality and original content, which will allow them to score with their
  followers.

- **The CONNECTOR** > grow his/her network

  A connector is as strong as his/her network. You can help expand this network by mentioning him/her in your own online network. Offline you can offer introductions to other influential voices in your sector.

- **The PERSONAL BRAND** > offer opportunities to strengthen his/her reputation and visibility.

  Like your brand, the image of a personal brand is sacred. Look for ways to strengthen this image; preferably in ways that will be seen by as many people as possible.

- **The ANALYST** > offer new data and insights.

  An analyst can never get enough facts, figures and knowledge. But be careful. Be generous with providing data, but don't do the analysis for him/her.

- **The ACTIVIST** > offer greater involvement in the conversation.

  Activists are often critical of brands and companies. You can make a good impression with them if you do not avoid this confrontational aspect, but offer instead to enter into dialogue with them. Failure to do this will only push them further away.

- **The EXPERT** > offer to share his/her expertise via your network.

  An expert likes to be seen to be an expert. Keep him/her informed of innovations and other news in your sector and give him/her a platform to share his/her knowledge with your customers and supporters.

- **The INSIDER** > offer the opportunity for constructive debate.

  An insider will usually have different interests and priorities to your own. Even so, you can still build up a fruitful relationship by agreeing to a constructive debate on the issues that separate you. This will give both sides the opportunity to spread their message.

- **The INNOVATOR** > offer information that can take innovative debate to the next level.

  An innovator is always on the lookout for new people who dare to brainstorm and to dream. Offer him/her essential information that can stimulate new discussions, which can potentially lead to disruptive innovations.

- **The JOURNALIST** > offer him/her scoops.

  The holy grail for every journalist is a scoop. If you can offer him/her a regular supply of this 'drug', his/her readers will also become addicted to his/her articles.

INSIGHT

> **UZ Brussels invites influencers to join the fight against corona**

During the corona crisis, hospitals have also discovered the communicative power of influencers. Because young people in large cities are often the most difficult to reach via traditional media, the University Hospital in Brussels invited a number of influencers to visit their COVID-19 wards. What they saw there made such a deep impression on them that they were immediately prepared to share their experiences.

On which channels should you use your influencers?

You can find influencers – and their networks – on a wide variety of channels. Almost every social network has its own influencers. But this does not mean that, as a brand, you need to be active on every platform. Just follow your target group. If your (potential) customers are not on LinkedIn, there is not much point in you being on it either. Are you trying to promote a new drink for young people? You probably need to add Snapchat to your media mix.

The form of your content also plays a role. Sometimes the value of a service can be made clearer in a video than in a photo. In that case, you would opt for YouTube in preference to Instagram as your channel of choice. If you are interested in spreading longish blog texts, you are better off using the platforms where the sharing of these kinds of texts is popular, like Facebook or Twitter.

Three platform-transcending trends

Last but not least, it is important for influencer marketeers to keep abreast of all the latest digital evolutions. The following three trends in social media are certain to have a major impact on influencer content in the years ahead.

1. The importance of mobile

People had been predicting it for years, but in 2016 it finally happened. In that year for the very first time, heavyweights like Facebook and Google received the majority of their visitors on mobile devices. This meant that all these people saw their influencer content on small screens, often while they were on the move. Anyone who takes this into account and best exploits this mini-format is likely to gain a serious advantage over his/her competitors.

2. Declining organic reach

It is becoming increasingly difficult for brands and influencers to reach all their followers 'organically': in other words, free of charge. Nowadays, you can only achieve this reach with paid advertising. This is a strategy that seems to be working to the benefit of Facebook and co.

3. Virtual reality

Virtual reality has come of age. Both Facebook (Oculus Rift) and Google (Google Daydream) are now mass-producing VR headsets. If you can succeed in being one of the first to surf on the wave of 360 degree video and other similar mind-blowing applications, your approach will be future-proof for several years to come and will leave your rivals standing.

These, then, are the essentials of influencer marketing. I hope that the reading of this chapter has whetted your appetite to start your own influencer marketing campaign. If you need any more information, I suggest you look at my book *Influencers*.

As has already been mentioned, early investment in an influencer network will give you a source of information about new trends that are likely to emerge in your sector, which will mean in turn (and more crucially) that you will be in a better position to gain faster and more accurate insights into the changing situation when the Zoonotic sandstorm finally erupts.

#NOMAKEUPSELFIE JOINS THE FIGHT AGAINST BREAST CANCER

Why would a huge number of women suddenly start posting selfies of themselves without make-up on social media? The answer is that they wanted to show their support for the fight against breast cancer. To each of their photos the women attached the hashtags #nomakeupselfie and #cancerawareness.

1. What is the creative idea and who benefits from it?

Cancer Research UK, an organisation that supports cancer research, noticed the emergence of the 'no make-up' trend and developed an idea to use it to raise funds for their work. They encouraged people to post a selfie of themselves without make-up and to make a £3 donation to the cause. After just 24 hours, Cancer Research UK had already collected almost £1 million. After another 24 hours, this amount had been doubled.

2. What stimulates people to share the idea?

The fact that 'the selfie' was then the buzzword of the year (2014) certainly helped to ensure the rapid spread of the idea. At the height of the campaign, some ten thousand tweets per day were posted with a hashtag. At a deeper level, however, the campaign gave people a good feeling about themselves. It was about self-affirmation, self-confidence and authenticity. The sharing of this message generated emotion. It created the sense of being part of a larger movement.

3. How can you use time pressure to speed up the process?

In this case, the process was speeded up by the fast reactions of Cancer Research UK. When they noted that an increasing number of women were posting selfies of themselves without make-up on various social media channels, they quickly picked up and exploited the viral trend, suggesting the addition of the hashtags #nomakeupselfie

UNDER THE
MICROSCOPE

and #cancerawareness, as well as the donation of £3 per photo. You don't always have to manipulate time pressure. Often, it is enough to be ready to jump on board the fast-moving trend as soon as it emerges. Providing, of course, you have a Cheetah mentality.

4. How do you get the support of big names?

Celebrities like Beyoncé, Jessica Alba and Rihanna all took part voluntarily.

5. How can you use short and memorable videos or photos?

Making a selfie without make-up requires very little time and effort, but it stimulates a huge amount of curiosity, because the women in question were willing to make themselves vulnerable and show it to the world.

6. How does this campaign motivate altruism?

The campaign encouraged people to leave their comfort zone, whilst at the same time recognising their support for a good cause. It was also pitched in such a way that it was easy to encourage your friends to take part.

7. How can you ensure that the threshold to participate is as low as possible?

It was very easy to take part in the challenge. All you needed was a smartphone and all you had to do was take a selfie. Nor did it require any kind of 'crazy' behaviour. You didn't have to dress up, or dance, or pour a bucket of water over your head.

Even so, this campaign also attracted its fair share of criticism. The critics said that the comparison between no make-up and cancer was inappropriate. Losing your hair and eyebrows as a result of cancer treatment is immeasurably more confrontational than a day without lipstick and mascara. However, these reflections did little to stop the trend. A growing number of both women and men took part. The men did the very opposite of the women: they posted photos of themselves wearing full make-up. In total, the campaign raised more than £8 million. Some people involved with cancer regarded the campaign as a flop, because the word 'cancer' was never once mentioned. But this is as ridiculous as saying that a blog is a flop simply because it does not specifically mention the name of the product it is intended to push. Such comments demonstrate a very poor knowledge of the essentials of marketing. The essence is not what moves you as the seller of a product or idea, but what moves your target group: the buyers and participants. This is what makes campaigns like Movember and #Nomakeupselfie such excellent examples of successful inbound marketing campaigns. Without going to extremes, they succeeded in involving a large target group. Perhaps only a small percentage of the participants made a financial contribution. But 20 percent of 1million is still always better than 80 percent of 100,000. If you are afraid of negative feedback, you will be unlikely to try out the new and innovative ideas that can often bring this kind of real success. And if all you want to do is win people's approval, you will never think of this kind of idea anyway.

2

NAVIGATING IN THE SANDSTORM

Once a Zoonotic attack reaches full power, all the other companies in the sector will find themselves engulfed in a blinding sandstorm, as the Cheetah rushes across the savannah.

Even Bill Gates admitted in his podcast that he allowed himself to be surprised by COVID-19, even though he had warned against the possibility of a pandemic in a TED Talk as long ago as 2015. In his opinion, the importance of face masks was grossly underestimated during the early phases of infection, because it was thought that corona, like a classic flu virus, was primarily spread through coughing and sneezing. It was only when it was later discovered just how important aerosols were for spreading the disease and just how much damage a Superspreader could cause in an enclosed and poorly ventilated space that the protective value of face masks, even in their most simple form, was finally recognised.

This illustrates that no matter how well prepared you think you might be, predicting a Zoonotic – never mind fighting one off – is always a perilous undertaking.

A veritable sandstorm is raging across the savannah
and you need to navigate in almost zero visibility.

For this reason, it is crucial that you and your team should practice what to do, long before the sandstorm engulfs you. This will put you in the best possible position to react coolly and calmly when all hell finally breaks loose.

EXPERT OPINION

Bill Gates

Microsoft
Bill and Melinda Gates Foundation

Are we ready for a pandemic?

It is interesting to look back at the TED Talk that Bill Gates gave in 2015, with what we now know and have experienced during the corona crisis at the back of our minds. Gates came onto the podium wheeling a trolley, on which stood a large barrel. It was the kind of barrel that many people had in their cellars during the 1950s and 1960s, when it contained what was supposedly necessary to survive a nuclear attack. 'But today,' said Gates, 'the danger does not come from nuclear missiles but from microbes and viruses,' following which he showed everyone an image of a corona-like virus.

He went on to add the prophetic words that the greatest danger of all would come from a respiratory virus, because this kind of virus could spread so quickly that many people would be infected before they ever displayed signs of symptoms. This is in contrast, for example, to ebola, when a person only becomes infectious when he/she is already dying, and even then only through contact with infected blood. This means that it is possible for doctors to respond more quickly to ebola, which in part explains why the disease has never been able to spread to large urban agglomerations and has never been able to cause a pandemic. Gates's TED talk should have been a wake-up call to prepare ourselves in time to meet 'The Big One', because 'time is not on our side'. His suggestions for preparing for this unpredictable future were:

1. Effective data surveillance systems: measuring and analysing what is happening via testing and contact tracing.
2. The training of a well-prepared team of professionals via war games, who would also be given the necessary tools and budget to treat the disease and develop vaccines.

In view of our experiences in recent times, I would add a third crucial suggestion:

3. Develop a focused target group communication strategy with unity of command.

These three action points are also relevant if you wish to prepare an effective defence against a viral business Zoonotic.

Who wields the hammer? Who leads the dance?

In March 2020, Tomas Pueyo, a Spanish-French data analyst, sketched in his blog a possible strategy for successfully dealing with the COVID-19 pandemic. The title of his blog was: 'The hammer and the dance'. What the next 18 months can look like, if leaders buy us time. At the time of writing, this article has been viewed more than 40 million times.

The importance of his contribution is not confined to the clear and easy-to-understand imagery of its 'hammer and dance' title. The sub-title is equally (if not more) important and revealing, because it emphasises the key role of the policy-makers. It may well be the case that Pueyo's suggested approach is more feasible in more authoritarian and/or more disciplined countries. Drastic measures without strong enforcement have little effect. Experience has shown that a tragedy often first needs to occur before there is widespread societal approval for wielding the hammer firmly.

It is possible to see the same scenario being played out in companies, where initially only a few people are aware of the true scale and nature of the approaching Zoonotic, while the majority continue to disbelieve the threat and wait passively or even actively oppose countermeasures.

In this respect, I would ask you to consider the following three crucial questions. And consider them now, not tomorrow:

1. Who are the people in your company who have the authority and power to decide that the hammer needs to be used? What would that hammer look like?
2. Who will lead the communication to motivate everyone within the organisation, so that the hammer can do its work?
3. If that is successful, who will lead the dance, which can sometimes last for months or even years?

THE HAMMER AND THE DANCE

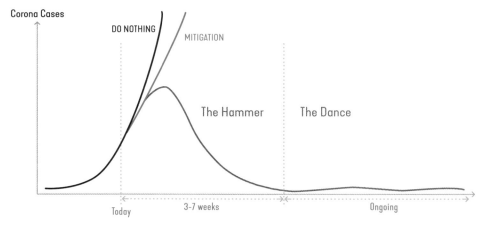

Source: Tomas Pueyo

Apple is an example of a company that successfully fought off a potential Zoonotic by incorporating an mp3 player into the iPhone, which allowed iTunes to be an effective strategy to neutralise Napster. In a similar vein, some observers think that if Netflix wants to become the Amazon of the entertainment field it really needs to include Spotify in its offer. Aware of this, Disney has successfully managed to get a serious foot in the door of the streaming market in response to the rapid growth of their Netflix rivals. Launched in 2019, by the end of 2020 Disney+ already had 87 million paying subscribers, whereas its original target was 90 million by 2024. As a result, they have now adjusted their 2024 target to no fewer than 260 million subscribers. In comparison, Netflix needed ten years to achieve its current customer base of 200 million.

In Flanders, the telecom provider Telenet and the broadcasters Vier and VRT have collaborated on the development of their own Streamz platform, in an effort to slow down the march of Netflix. At the moment, it is not yet clear whether this strategy will succeed. It will all depend on whether they can exploit the Unfair Advantage of Streamz in a more focused manner.

If your company finds itself in a Zoonotic sandstorm, this will create fear, unease and stress. When this happens, it is crucial that the leaders demonstrate agility and resilience. With this in mind, I asked Professor Elke Van Hoof for her advice about how best to achieve this calm response. I first met Elke at a conference in the far north of Finland and there was an immediate click between us. I value her for her no-nonsense, 'to the point' style, based on her outstanding knowledge and many years of practical experience.

I can recognise myself all too clearly in Elke's wise words. In my organisation, I am also often the hen that walks ahead of the brood, with my gaze focused on the future, but I also keep my eyes and ears open for the concerns of my team behind me. And, like her, I also 'clear my shit' by intense training sessions for a marathon I hope to run. For me, this purifies both body and mind.

EXPERT OPINION

Prof. Dr Elke Van Hoof

Huis voor Veerkracht (House for Resilience)
Senior lecturer, Free University of Brussels

'Clear your shit'

'Dealing constructively with a crisis requires more than resilience alone. That is just one element of the solution. You cannot separate resilience from its context, because this context can either hinder or facilitate resilience. A person's resilience is part of a wider concept that I call the activation quotient. This activation quotient determines the extent to which people are capable of action, innovation, creativity and progress. It is a combination of your resilience on the one hand and your ambition on the other hand; the extent to which you feel safe or connected and are ready make an effort in a given situation. For example, a person might have a high degree of resilience, but if his ambition in a situation is low then the effort he makes will also be low. It is the activation quotient that ultimately determines your level of agility.

This agility demands a good physical condition. You must be in sufficiently good shape to make a serious and sustained effort. But you also need the right mindset, a mindset where you are not fighting against something, but rather for something: for your idea, your vision. If you can detach this from your ego, you will become super-agile. Sadly, however, I often see that the ego continues to get in the way, especially in the higher echelons of organisations. Senior managers are all too frequently concerned with preserving the status quo and feeding their ego, so that they constantly compare themselves with others. Whereas an agile leader stays first and foremost in contact with his own inner strength.

You can learn agility, but it takes a great deal of effort. I refer to this as "clearing your shit". As long as you remain trapped by your ego, you will continue to be locked into a painful situation, a trauma from the past. That is paradoxical, because many new products and service are developed precisely because of a dissatisfaction with the here and now, with what currently exists. Once you get started, you must be able to free yourself from that old pain.

Someone who has cleared his shit is someone who dares to be authentic. He dares to let himself be seen and is not afraid to talk about his past shit. He is willing to admit that things don't always run smoothly each and every day.

A strong leader also realises that his behaviour must set a good example, because the chicks always follow the mother hen. But the hen must never forget to stay in touch with the chicks trailing along behind, by responding promptly to their cheep-cheep.

The corona crisis was also a difficult period for me, and one in which I was constantly asked to give advice: by the government, the care centres, the business world and goodness knows who else. I was only able to keep up this frantic pace by taking exercise every day and by planning a "clear my shit" day once a month. I would recommend it to everyone.'

What has corona taught us?

In his podcast for *De Tijd* newspaper, Peter Piot, a microbiologist, director of the London School of Hygiene and Tropical Medicine and also an expert in AIDS and ebola, detailed a number of things we have already learned from corona about the best way to fight a virus. Much of his advice can also be very useful in a business context.

- **Leave your comfort zone**

  We need to think in terms of totally new models. A good example is the search for a COVID-19 vaccine. In addition to following the tried and trusted paths for developing classic flu vaccines, which are designed to stimulate the immune system, scientists are also now working on an entirely new approach based on RNA, which stimulates the body to make its own vaccine. The vaccines of Pfizer and BioNTech, which are 95 percent effective, both make use of this technique.

- **Work together across boundaries**

  This is another area where the search for a vaccine is a good example. Not only was the DNA of the virus quickly shared worldwide, but scientists have also exchanged other valuable information across the boundaries of countries and companies.

- **Unity of command and communication**

  The complex structure of national authorities and contrasting political visions have all too often ensured that decisions were not taken or were taken too late. The virus makes grateful use of any lack of leadership and a divide-and-rule communication style.

- **One team, one goal**

  A silo structure and an 'I, me, mine' culture are diametrically opposed to the 'we, us, our' culture that is necessary to deal with the crisis. According to Piot, this is one of the reasons why Asian countries have succeeded in getting the virus under control more quickly. In Japan, for example, the wearing of a face mask for something as banal as a common cold has been standard practice for decades. People do this uncomplainingly to protect others.

- **Sense of urgency**

  The previously mentioned steps can only take place if everyone in the community feels a sufficient sense of urgency. We now know that previously made plans are generally of little value once the crisis breaks. But the planning process itself continues to be highly valuable.

- **Build and maintain dykes**

  The Dutch learnt important lessons from the many disastrous floods they experienced in the past. They have invested heavily in the building and strengthening of coastal dykes and other water management measures. This costs huge amounts of time and money, but it is crucial that everything is maintained in good condition, so that the defences can do their job properly the next time another massive storm hits – as it undoubtedly will.

- **This is going to last for some time**

  We need to assume that the virus will still be with us for quite some time to come. According to Piot, medical science has so far only ever succeeded in eradicating just a single virus: polio. Most other viruses, such as smallpox and AIDS, are still with us, although happily we now have vaccines that allow us to control them.

EXPERT OPINION

Philippe De Backer

Politician Open VLD
Former minister during the first corona wave

The right man in the right place

With his background as a doctor in the biotechnology sector, Philippe De Backer was the right man in the right place at the right time during the first wave of the corona pandemic in Belgium. No one was better equipped to ensure the necessary ramping up of testing capacity and to organise the efficient purchase and distribution of the necessary materials to combat the disease. In short, he was the ideal person to respond in the best possible way to the Zoonotic attack. Is it just a coincidence that his approach demonstrated the seven key traits of a Cheetah?

'To deal effectively with an unexpected pandemic with the necessary sense of urgency, you first need to have the right data and the right mindset that will allow you to estimate what an exponential rate of growth can really mean. That is by no means self-ev-ident, as can be seen from the fact that even experienced virologists were forced to admit afterwards that they had also underestimated the infectiousness and the speed of this virus.

The main challenge as a leader in this situation is being able to deal with uncertainty, coping with the fact that you do not have enough exact information about the current position in a reality that is constantly changing from day to day and even from hour to hour.

I decided to approach the pandemic in the same way that I would approach setting up a start-up.

First, I quickly removed a number of barriers between a dozen or so of the relevant services and made sure that everyone was fully involved. From the very beginning, we decided on five very clear targets: more testing, more protective materials, more medical materials, more medicines and the better organisation of the necessary logistics in the field.

Ensuring good communication between all those involved is just as important. Every morning at seven o'clock we held an online meeting of team leaders to agree on the action points for the day ahead and we had a further meeting at six o'clock each evening to discuss what we had achieved. This fixed structure with clear benchmarks provided a reassuring degree of transparency and calm, notwithstanding the chaotic nature of the situation.

Something else that is essential when dealing with a previously unknown crisis of this kind is that you make quick use of your network. When it became clear that the private laboratories were unable to deal with more than 5,000 tests per day, whereas our original target was 10,000 tests, I immediately used my contacts in the pharmaceutical and biotechnology sectors. With just a few telephone calls, I was able to mobilise various experts, universities and private companies to organise the necessary expansion of our testing capacity within 48 hours. We also decided to make use of a German protocol for the automation of the test procedure, so that we could increase the volume more quickly. Of course, we also needed to find the necessary equipment to make this possible. The normal delivery period was a number of weeks or even months, so to overcome this we contacted all the laboratories and biotech companies that were closed because of the lockdown to ask them if we could 'borrow' their equipment and centralise it in five different test centres spread around the country. In this way, we were quickly able to organise significantly more tests per head of population than, for example, our colleagues in The Netherlands and Germany.

Very few people know that all these companies agreed to cooperate voluntarily and that we were not asked to pay anything, except the cost of the reagents. They all regarded it as a service to their country.

In this kind of situation, you also need to ensure that you involve people who have the right competencies, even if you have to find them outside your own organisation. For example, the government has no experience of buying specialised medical material on the international market in such large quantities and in such a short space of time. Government departments are used to working with public tender procedures, but these can last for months, which was out of the question in the middle of a crisis. As a result, I immediately decided to make use of experts in the field who are familiar with the complexities of international purchasing processes.

Finally, a major logistical tour de force was necessary to ensure that all these materials got to the right place as quickly as possible. For this, I decided to call in the army.

Distributing medical material in this way was a bit like trying to set up bol.com in 48 hours!

The best way to avoid a repetition of this kind of chaos in the future is to make sure that you are well prepared in advance and that you have at your disposal at least a strategic supply of the necessary protective and medical materials. It is also necessary to carry out regular simulation exercises, so that you can be sure, for example, that the emergency services are capable of dealing with all contingencies.

Of course, this all costs money, but our experiences in 2020 have taught us – as they have also taught the rest of the world – that not being prepared costs even more. An awful lot more. An added complication is the fact that the division of competencies in our country is highly complex and fragmented. This is something that can only be improved by structural reform.

In the meantime, we have now anchored all the relevant procedures in a plan, but even that is worth very little unless it is regularly practised and amended where necessary.'

I regard this testimony by Philippe De Backer as a wake-up call that invites you to think about what I described in my previous book as the seven advantages of the Cheetah:

1. **Speed** – What barriers and silos in your organisation can hinder a fast and appropriate response?
2. **Focus** – How can you ensure that you remain abreast of evolutions and potential threats inside and, above all, outside your sector? Do not be obsessive, but make sure that your company culture encourages speed and agility.
3. **Story** – What story can you use to overcome resistance inside your organisation and increase engagement?
4. **Agility** – How well do you function in situations of great uncertainty, in which things are continually changing or are, by definition, unpredictable?
5. **Territory** – Where, if necessary, can you quickly gain access to experts and find the other resources you need, both inside and outside your company or country?
6. **Resources** – Have you developed the necessary Zoonotic prevention scenarios and, preferably, tested them?
7. **Network** – Who can you call at every hour of the day or night to help you when the going gets tough? Have you invested in your network before you really need to make use of it? Do you know and have you established good relations with your influencers before you need them?

Is a Zoonotic initially difficult to identify?

Sometimes you can see a Zoonotic emerging, but do not yet have the resources to react or else you react in the wrong way. The first thing you need to do is to monitor how the Zoonotic unfolds its strategy. A Zoonotic usually focuses on a single or a limited number of objectives. However, it is not always easy to identify those objectives. On the contrary, it is often very difficult to spot a Zoonotic competitor in your market.

Although experts are constantly issuing warnings about the approach of Zoonotics, very few organisations are prepared for their arrival. In this respect, it is ironic perhaps that New York, the epicentre of the corona crisis in the United States, had actually carried out a pandemic simulation exercise just four months before

the real pandemic broke (which later gave plenty of ammunition to the conspiracy theorists, but also proved that even if you have taken precautions a Zoonotic
can still strike hard). As with 9/11, New York owed its recovery to the resilience
of its citizens. They didn't lose heart and sit around doing nothing. Instead, they
reacted with Cheetah-like speed. And it was the same story in October 2012, when
some of my friends who were in the city for the annual marathon witnessed at
first hand the toughness and durability of the New Yorkers in response to the
sudden arrival of Hurricane Sandy. Perhaps you need this kind of resilience simply to survive from day to day in one of the most hectic and competitive cities in
the world!

If a Zoonotic is ready to burst into your market, you may perhaps notice that some
of your KPIs are on the downturn, without there being any obvious explanation.
You should take this as a first signal to get ready for the storm. If you have not
taken precautions to anticipate events, you can only respond to them when they
happen, which immediately puts you in a much weaker position. Although you
may have been aware of the potential danger of a Zoonotic, there is a good chance
that your organisation will have focused its attention too strongly inwards, instead of looking outwards; too much on your own sector and not enough on what
was happening elsewhere.

The approach of the COVID-19 Taskforce in the port of Antwerp

As a member of the board of directors of the Port Authority, I saw for myself how
a large and complex organisation was able to react to the unpredictable. As the
second largest port in Europe, Antwerp is a hugely important artery for the Belgian
economy: more than 300 scheduled services operating to more than 800 destinations ensure a worldwide connectivity. Each year, the port handles some 238 million tons of international maritime trade and is also home to the largest integrated
chemical cluster in Europe. Its harbour provides, directly or indirectly, something
like 143,000 jobs and creates an added value in excess of 20 billion euros. The Antwerp Port Authority itself employs some 1,600 personnel.

Because the port is essential for the supply lines not only of Belgium but also for much of Europe, it was crucial that the harbour facilities should remain 100 percent operational during the lockdown. The port's COVID-19 Taskforce was charged with making this possible. Various chains in the port's organisation were immediately involved, so that the taskforce was both multi-disciplinary and transboundary. The Joint Nautical Authority was also represented, because of its role in ensuring accessibility to the port via the River Scheldt.

The taskforce, which met weekly, defined the following list of key issues that needed to be constantly monitored:

1. Identifying and settling differences

   The approach to COVID-19 in Belgium differed from the approach in The Netherlands. However, the pilots on the Scheldt included men and women from both countries. The Dutch authorities used a different set of rules from their Belgian/Flemish counterparts. Following joint consultation, an approach was agreed to ensure that the two sets of rules were not contradictory.

2. Maintaining staffing levels

   The availability of sufficient personnel is essential for the effective functioning of the harbour. Various absence scenarios were developed to guarantee the unbroken provision of all services.

3. Ensuring health and safety

   A set of basic rules was drawn up and implemented:
   - Providing sufficient cleaning materials and disinfectants in machines.
   - Making the transfer of documents as digital as possible, to restrict direct human contact to a minimum.
   - Ensuring that communication between ships' crews and quayside personnel took place as far as possible at a safe distance (via radio, telephone, etc.).
   - Applying the social distancing rules wherever possible and, in particular, keeping 1.5 metres between all personnel (ship and quayside).

EXPERT OPINION

Bert Brugghemans
Commander, Antwerp Fire Department

'Trust the process'

As the commander of the Antwerp Fire Department, Bert Brugghemans is well placed to give his opinion about how best to deal with a crisis. One thing is for certain: he does not believe in the value of written crisis plans, precisely because its unpredictability is the essential characteristic of a real crisis. Instead, he puts his faith in a clearly developed understanding of the process that needs to be followed.

'The first step of the process is to get a clear idea of what is going on. What has happened? What is the problem? You cannot respond to a crisis with classic cause-and-effect logic, which follows a reasonably predicable path. A crisis is total chaos, which means that the relationship between cause and effect is no longer quite so obvious. The most well-known example is the butterfly that flaps its wings in the Amazon rain forest and causes a hurricane in the Philippines.

But what people often forget to mention with this example is that the butterfly has probably flapped its wings hundreds of times before without causing a hurricane. Or to put it in slightly different terms: there are so many other contextual factors that also play a role in a crisis. Above all, you need to be aware of the remarkable and unique context in which you find yourself at that particular moment.

The worst thing that you can do in this kind of situation is to sit in a meeting room for a few hours (or days) to debate which approach is 'best'. It is much more important to act quickly and to learn iteratively than to rely on a consultative model that has been drawn up in advance. To use military parlance, there is a need to act in "battle rhythm": you discuss briefly, act quickly and then discuss again after an agreed

period, so that you can make adjustments on the basis of what you have learnt. This process is then repeated until the situation is under control. You let your experts do their work and use their insights and experience to constantly amend and improve your approach.

Act fast, learn fast, adjust fast: that is the essence.

When a fire starts, for example, the teams on the spot consult with each other for five minutes every quarter of an hour, so that their approach to the blaze can be coordinated. As the fire is brought increasingly under control, the consultation rhythm is slowed down.

As already mentioned, letting your experts do their work is another important condition for successfully dealing with a crisis. The corona crisis was a good example of this. To act effectively, input was needed from various experts: virologists, motivational psychologists, vaccination specialists, bio-statisticians, etc. Because experts have the tendency to remain strictly within the confines of their domain, co-ordinating their various activities on a regular basis is crucial, so that the overall approach can be adjusted accordingly, even if all the analyses and data are not fully available.

Some people argued for the need for unity of control based on the "command and control" principle, but that is an approach that dates back to the Napoleonic era, when two clearly defined armies stood opposed to each other. Today's crises are so complex that they are impossible to control with this simple principle. A central command headquarters causes delay. You need to give control to your experts on the ground, who can see the situation at first hand. You must give them the necessary freedom, within certain agreed limits, to take the decisions they think are necessary. This is called "frontline command". I am also a great believer in a coordinated approach based on the "swarm principle", as a result of which each bird constantly adjusts its flight to match those of its fellow birds, based on a few simple ground rules, such as keeping a minimum distance, not bumping into your neighbour, etc. This is a highly flexible approach that ensures continuous adaptation to ever-changing circumstances. There is no one leader in a swarm; everyone plays their role. Although it was originally thought that this approach was above all suitable for complex crises, research carried out in The Netherlands now suggests that it works well in all situations, including "simple" crises.

During a crisis many people seem to feel the need for a single, strong and clearly identifiable leader, but in reality that is a utopian idea. In a crisis what you really need is distributed leadership, although it must be tightly coordinated. For this, you certainly need someone who can firmly control the coordination process, someone who can succeed in letting and getting the experts to work together harmoniously. Communicating with the outside world does not necessarily always need to be done by the same person, as long as the core message and its tone remain the same. The most important thing is to ensure that you reach all your target groups.

My most important piece of advice: "Trust the process", but make sure that the coordination measures are clearly defined in advance and regularly practiced.'

AN EXAMPLE OF A CRISIS CONSULTATION MODEL

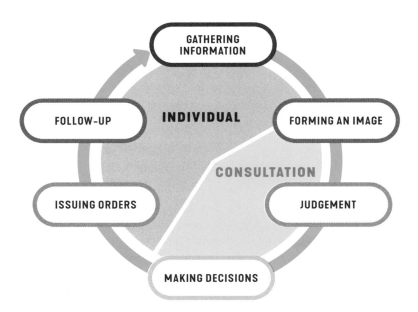

Source: *IBOBBO-model 'Help! A crisis'* – Bruelemans, Brugghemans & Van Mechelen – 2015 die Keure

IBOBBO is a Dutch acronym. The IBOBBO model stands for:

- Information gathering: this is necessary to form a correct picture of the situation. However, this phase is not endless. It only continues until enough information has been collected to make a decision.
- Forming an image: in any consultation process having a clear image of what you are discussing is crucial. This means that the information that has been gathered must be structured at each level (on the spot, in the immediate vicinity and in the wider vicinity).
- Forming a judgement: on the basis of the current image of the situation, a number of actions need to be determined, which means making choices in relation to an agreed order of priorities.
- Making decisions: good decisions ensure an assertive, efficient and safe direction of events.
- Issuing orders: in a crisis, orders can be issued either on the basis of a command model or a coordination structure.
- Follow-up: this is a very important phase for which the lead time must be kept short. Without prompt and accurate follow-up, decisions risk being taken by others who do not have an overall picture of the situation.

The IBOBBO model is not just a crisis management model, but can also be seen as a quality control model, a guidance model and an information management model. During a crisis, it is important to work efficiently and effectively, which also means ensuring quality and giving guidance. Likewise, the flow of information is one of the biggest problems in any crisis, so that it is important that the model you use takes account of this aspect.

CHILD FOCUS AND #CATSFORKIDS

On the Day for the Protection of Children Against Sexual Abuse, Child Focus, working in collaboration with Wunderman Thompson Antwerp, launched a new awareness campaign. Hats off to the team under the leadership of Erwin Jansen. They found a very accessible way to turn the spotlight on this highly charged subject. How? By encouraging people to share photographs of cats as a symbolic way to show support for the campaign to give greater protection to vulnerable children. Each day an average of roughly 243,000 photos of cats were shared. Sadly, the number of online photographs depicting child sexual abuse is estimated at 19 million, which is 78 times more than the daily number of shared cat photos.

The media plan made use of sponsored posts on Facebook and Instagram, collaboration with influencers, and flyers in pet shops to promote the visibility of the campaign. Moreover, it was not just 'ordinary' influencers who took part; a number of cat-owning celebrities also shared photos of their favourite feline friends.

1. **What is the creative idea and who benefits from it?**

   The proposal came from Wunderman Thompson. Child Focus appealed online for people to post photographs of cats accompanied by a handwritten message: 'For every cat photo shared online, there are 78 photos of child sexual abuse'.

2. **What stimulates people to share the idea? What are the memorable buzzwords or hashtags?**

   Cat photos are always popular on social media. These photos, in combination with the handwritten annotation and the hashtag #catsforkids, gave the message extra power.

3. **How can you use time pressure to speed up the process?**

   Child Focus used the worldwide attention generated by the Day for the Protection of Children Against Sexual Abuse to give a boost to the launch of this awareness campaign, which created the necessary pressure right from the very start.

4. How do you get the support of big names and how do you find a match with important influencers?

The media plan that Wunderman Thompson created for Child Focus made use of sponsored posts on Facebook and Instagram, collaboration with influencers, and flyers in pet shops to promote the visibility of the campaign. Moreover, it was not just 'ordinary' influencers who took part; a number of cat-owning celebrities also shared photos of their favourite feline friends.

5. How can you use a short and memorable image or video?

Cats have been hugely popular on social media right from the very start. I sometimes say as a joke that the CEO of the internet is probably a cat! For many people, cats have a magnetic attraction and they are an endless source for creative InstaStories, TikTok messages and millions of YouTube hits.

6. How does this campaign motivate and demonstrate engagement and altruism?

The cat photos on which this campaign is based are an accessible way to focus attention on what is a highly charged subject. It is a playful manner by which to publically show to other people your concern for and commitment to the vulnerable.

7. How can you ensure that the threshold to participate is kept as low as possible?

Many people are willing to post photos of cats online quicker than you can say 'meow'. It doesn't get much more low-threshold than that!

3

WHAT IS YOUR ZOONOTIC DEFENCE SCENARIO?

The Zoonotic has begun its exponential breakthrough. Draconian measures are required. But never forget that panic is a bad adviser.

Your challenge is to put together a fire brigade,
while the fire is already raging.

Recognising the different phases of the attack

When a pandemic breaks out, the World Health Organisation (WHO) uses a colour code to categorise the seriousness of the infection level in the different phases. You can use a comparable model in the business world to analyse a Zoonotic attack.

WHO PANDEMIC INFLUENZA PHASES

PHASE	DESCRIPTION
Phase 1	No animal influenza virus circulating among animals has been reported to cause infection in humans.
Phase 2	An animal influenza virus circulating in domesticated or wild animals is known to have caused infection in humans and is therefore considered a specific potential pandemic threat.
Phase 3	An animal or human-animal influenza reassortant virus has caused sporadic cases or small clusters of disease in people, but has not resulted in human-to-human transmission sufficient to sustain community-level outbreaks.
Phase 4	Human-to-human transmission of an animal or human-animal influenza reassortant virus able to sustain community-level outbreaks has been verified.
Phase 5	Human-to-human spread of the virus in two or more countries in one WHO region.
Phase 6	In addition to the criteria defined in Phase 5, the same virus spreads from human to human in at least one other country in another WHO region.
Post peak period	Levels of pandemic influenza in most countries with adequate surveillance have been dropped below peak levels.
Post pandemic period	Levels of influenza activity have returned to the levels seen for seasonal influenza in most countries with adequate surveillance.

PHASE 1	DENIAL (LIGHT BLUE)	The first signs of an approaching Zoonotic are visible, but you do not think they are significant enough to devote further attention to them.
PHASE 2	UNDERESTIMATION (LIGHT RED)	Your attention to the signals increases, but you still underestimate the Zoonotic's potential danger of exponential growth.
PHASE 3	CONTROL (RED)	You at last recognise the danger and take measures that are intended to control the Zoonotic and limit the damage.
PHASE 4	CONSUMED (BLUE)	The fight is over. The Zoonotic has devoured you and pushed you out of your market.

Fast tracing and reporting

Good predictive models, which can indicate how the viral business strategy of the Zoonotic might evolve, are extremely useful. You need to develop the necessary systems that will allow you to gather as much material as quickly as possible, which will enable you to map out and follow the evolution of the Zoonotic. Make maximum use of the most up-to-date technology. This will make it possible for you, with the help of bots, to send questionnaires to all your staff, customers and suppliers, so that you can keep records of who replies and who does not. Bots also make it feasible to automatically follow moment by moment what is happening on social media.

By exploiting the potential of AI and machine learning in this way, you will be able to create order in your massive data stream, allowing you to identify hidden trends and to recognise certain patterns. Just as the Cheetah can see its prey and its enemies at a distance of five kilometres, so you will also be able to see what is approaching you much more quickly. Classic companies tend to do classic marketing research, such as panel discussions, focus groups and surveys. The new players and budding Zoonotics examine what the browsers and clicks tell them and observe the online behaviour of customers day after day. The mix of both methods gives the best results. Also remember to use your people in their different departments to serve as your eyes and ears in the marketplace. Above all, make sure that you do not limit your vision to just the local market. Never forget: a Zoonotic knows no boundaries.

Ensure that your reporting is made in compact, clear summaries or dashboards. By automating these processes to the maximum possible extent, you will free up time to concentrate on the quality of your day-to-day operations.

INSIGHT

> **Google Ventures**

During my visit to Googleplex in California, amongst those I met was the entrepreneur Rick Klau, who is responsible for Google Ventures, which is Google's incubator for new projects. His motto is:

'We invest in teams, not just ideas.'

This is an excellent attitude if you want to protect your existing business against potential Zoonotics. At the time of my visit, 300 of the 500 portfolio companies were still active. Of these, 25 had been launched on the stock market and had been sold to third parties, such as Apple, Facebook and even Monsanto.

Google Ventures is intended as an investment vehicle for the mother company, Alphabet. One of their projects makes it possible to write out the human genome in four hours at a cost of just one thousand dollars, whereas the first human attempt to achieve this feat took 14 years and cost one billion dollars. Another of their most celebrated ventures was Zipline, a spin-off from a failed toy company. In Rwanda, Zipline made it possible for crucial medical supplies and blood to be delivered quickly and safely throughout the country via drones.

According to Klau, there are three key factors that help to determine the success of Silicon Valley:
1. The availability of world-class education (including the universities at Stanford and Berkeley).
2. Sharp focus and grit.
3. Access to capital.

It is also useful that the legislation in California forbids the use of non-competition clauses, so that brilliant innovators have more freedom than elsewhere.

Reacting quickly

Perhaps you are successful in tracking down Client Zero: the innovators and the influencers. That is good, because it will give you a clearer picture about the profile of those who are most likely to be tempted by the offer of the new Zoonotic. Once you have found these people, you can then go in search of similar profiles in your customer portfolio, so that you can immediately start to develop a strategy that will increase their immunity to 'infection' by the Zoonotic.

Speed and agility are crucial qualities for resisting a Zoonotic attack. Just keeping your head down and hoping that the storm will pass is never going to work. It makes more sense, for example, to immediately make a beta-version of your new or amended product or service on a limited scale, so that you are then in a position, on the basis of your first experiences with it, to decide whether or not it is an effective strategy that can help in your Zoonotic defence. The development of a vaccine also happens in this same phased manner: from laboratory, through tests on animals, to clinical trials in humans, initially on a limited scale but with the intention of later extending this to a much larger group of people.

In the first weeks after the terrorist attacks of 9/11 in New York, General Motors immediately launched an incentive programme that encouraged Americans to keep on buying cars, seeing this as a way to support their personnel, dealers and suppliers. And this precisely at a moment when many other companies, worried by the uncertain situation, were putting on the brakes and introducing cost-cutting packages.

The following were the guidelines issued by the Association of National Advertisers to its members. They can apply equally to the corona crisis:
1. Take care of your people; give them the time and space to process their emotions.
2. Stay close to your customers and be alert to their fears and priorities; be aware that their moods and attitudes will be changing constantly.
3. Help consumers to regain confidence; this is important for our nation and our companies.
4. Be extra empathic in the tone and style of your communication; avoid images or jokes that might touch a nerve.
5. Prepare for a new future with a new normal; explore different possible scenarios.

INSIGHT

> **UiPath Health Screening Bot**

UiPath is a company specialising in the development of Robotic Process Automation (RPA). As soon as the first signs of the COVID-19 crisis became evident, the company launched an app to help companies in Asian and Pacific countries to carry out the health screening of their staff that had been made obligatory by the authorities. The bot sent, collected and analysed questionnaires to draw up reports on the daily health parameters (including temperature readings) of all relevant employees. People who did not fill in and return the questionnaire were automatically sent a reminder. In addition to the ready-made templates, the user companies also had the option to have the software adjusted to reflect their specific needs. The ease of use and the speed with which the critical data was collected made it possible even for companies with relatively limited means to keep operating safely and efficiently by allowing them to track down potentially infected employees. Are you also in a position to quickly collect the data you need to support your decision-making process?

Practise via a Zoonotic wargame

Preparation is the key for being ready when The Big One hits. When that happens, it is all hands on deck!

'Never ready, always prepared'.
Let that be your motto!

That is why I would argue that you need to carry out strategic exercises on a regular basis to simulate a Zoonotic attack in your sector in real time. You also need to set up a Zoonotic team that can assess the level of the potential threat. This team should play the role of market experts and business analysts who collect data about the consequences of a Zoonotic competitor somewhere in a distant market. Try to involve as many people from as many different departments and regions as possible, via a virtual forum where necessary. Confront the participants with hypothetical scenarios and let them think about how the Zoonotic could evolve into a serious threat. In this way, you teach your teams to remain resilient in unpredictable situations, so that when the real crisis breaks they will be able to assess the impact on your organisation and its systems.

You can compare a simulation with a vaccination: both prepare the immune system for an attack by a real Zoonotic virus.

ONE MORE THING

BOOK MARKET GROWTH

The arrival of Amazon, which started life as an online bookstore, was primarily detrimental to the independent booksellers. It is not that the sale of books has declined. Quite the reverse, although the pressure on publishers has increased dramatically, resulting in more and more mergers and scale-ups. In addition to growing sales for classic books and e-books, the pandemic also gave a serious boost to the sale of audiobooks. Of course, it is now abundantly clear that Amazon is so much more than an online bookstore. In 2020, it was also the fastest growing health company in the world. And there is every likelihood that they will soon become the digital guardian of healthcare, thanks in no small measure to the data they collect via their wearables. It is also likely that Amazon will not limit itself to the offer of appropriate products and services, such as dietary regimes and insurance. It seems more probable that the company will also want to provide diagnostic or even first line health services. 82 percent of American households already have a relationship of trust with Amazon. No other company comes anywhere close. And what is the most important factor in healthcare? Exactly. Trust.

Look at the emergency services and the armed forces. They not only draw up emergency plans for crises and disasters, but also repeatedly practise them in conditions that are as realistic as possible. You need to do the same with your Zoonotic war games, so that your team can practise their flexible thinking, based on the philosophy: 'Never ready, always prepared!' As a minimum, this kind of simulation exercise can be made part of an annual teambuilding session. But even more repetitions can certainly do you no harm. Quite the reverse.

What does it involve? Leaders of different business units come together to react in real time to hypothetical scenarios. The questions, decisions and possible consequences that arise out of this process are collected and conclusions drawn. The results will often speak for themselves and will help the participants to better understand how unprepared they are to meet the emergence of a Zoonotic competitor. Even a team with your very best people and a mix of ages, genders, years of service and geographical regions will be forced to reach that same conclusion, at least if they are honest with themselves. Be that as it may, conducting a simulation in advance is far preferable to testing a hypothesis in the heat of a Zoonotic battle. What's more, a simulation provides a framework for a more collective approach involving all your stakeholders and external partners.

- Step 1. Gather information: not only from your sector, but also from other sectors that might not at first glance seem related.
- Step 2. Identify trends: what are the coming hypes; what are the current uncertainties?
- Step 3. Estimate impact: rank the trends according to the likelihood that they will have an impact on your company.
- Step 4. Plan for different scenarios: think of possible reactions for the different situations you have identified.
- Step 5. Create teams: each team represents a possible competitor.
- Step 6. Play devil's advocate: let the teams debate with each other about their relative strengths and weaknesses for a number of rounds, under the supervision of a moderator.
- Step 7. Assess effects: ask all the teams to present their conclusions from the role-playing exercise.
- Step 8. Start again: initiate a new round of role-playing, based on the lessons learnt during the previous sessions.

INSIGHT

› Waymo turns the car industry on its head

Waymo is the company within the Alphabet group of Google that is responsible for the development of the self-driving car. I spoke with the then CFO, Gerard Dwyer, and was most impressed with the manner in which the company looks at the car business. They have a vision that is totally different from what you usually find in the sector. The essence of their approach can be summarised in a single sentence:

'We don't want to build cars, but we want to be the world's best driver.'

The company has already collected masses of data and knowledge about self-driving cars, based on 7 billion miles of simulated tests and 10 million miles on actual public roads in 25 cities throughout the United States.

Did you know that cars spend 95 percent of their time standing still? As a result, thousands and thousands of hectares of land are wasted for parking spaces. In Europe, the Middle East and Africa some 27,000 people are killed each year in traffic accidents; in 94 percent of these cases the cause was human error. Self-driving cars have the potential to correct this, as well as offering revolutionary new possibilities for people with visual impairments. These cars will also have an impact on hotels, the property sector, insurance, car parks and taxis, to name but a few. If you are active in one of these sectors, what is your defence strategy? You haven't got one? If I was you, I would start thinking about it NOW!

Here is an example of a defensive strategy based on wargames for the Novy company:

BUILD SCENARIOS FOR NOVY TO COMPETE

GATHER INFORMATION	IDENTIFYING	ASSESSMENT OF IMPACT	PLAN SEVERAL SCENARIOS
Understand and define Novy's strategic problems, objectives or uncertainties for Novy versus competition and channel conflict	Identify emerging trends, uncertainties and potential disruptions that may affect Novy's business	Assess these trends qualitatively to set them on a roadmap for Novy Evaluate and prioritise these trends by their potential impact and their degree of uncertainty before adding them to the action plan	Build scenarios to react and anticipate versus Novy's competitors and objectives

NEXT STEP: PUT YOUR SCENARIOS INTO A WAR GAME

TEAMS	ROLE-PLAYING	EFFECT	NEXT SESSION
Small groups, each representing a different player Example: Player 1: "Amazon" Player 2: Novy Player 3: Leicht Player 4: …	Involves a series of rounds that represent a specific period of time or phase in a plan All teams act concurrently at the same time without information on each other Use your scenarios	All teams analyse the output by presenting their work Evaluation of strengths and weaknesses, actions and decisions Arrival of early strategies	Additional session where Novy teams defeat again This is possible during the same day or weekend. It can also be a perfect Novy teambuilding All teams play again to make additional moves to win the battle

PREPARATION: HOW DO THEY REACT AND HOW DO WE IMPROVE?

Successful Zoonotic-busters react with lightning speed

The story of the husband and wife team Ugur Sahin and Özlem Türeci, founders of the German BioNTech pharmaceutical company, is a brilliant example of what I call Zoonotic-busting. Together with Pfizer, they helped to lay the foundations for the first and highly promising COVID-19 vaccine. Ugur Sahin is a professor of oncology and CEO of BioNTech. He started the company in 2008 with the intention of developing a new cancer therapy. Until he read an article in *The Lancet* about a virus in Wuhan. He quickly came to the conclusion that this virus would eventually lead to a pandemic and he felt that he had an obligation to try to respond to the threat.

The company's story illustrates the most important qualities of a Zoonotic-buster:

1. **Flexibility:** BioNTech immediately switched from searching for a vaccination against cancer to a vaccine that could beat the corona virus. Forty people were instantly allocated to the project. Whenever possible, all leave was cancelled. The company stimulated the working of overtime by offering generous compensation.

2. **Innovative thinking:** BioNTech used a totally new therapy, based on RNA. Innovation had been the focus of their work long before the outbreak of the pandemic. Innovation not necessarily to maximise market value, but innovation because they know that certain problems can only be solved with brilliant new ideas. That is their focus.

3. **Extreme speed:** BioNTech's project is named 'Lichtgeschwindigkeit' (Speed of Light) – and not without good reason. In a crisis, slowness can be fatal. It is impossible for you to become a Zoonotic or to fend one off unless you move at lightning speed.

This was a marvellous triumph for the 55-year-old Sahin, who came to Germany in the 1970s as the son of an immigrant worker from Turkey. He studied medicine, specialised in oncology, married another oncologist with Turkish roots and soon began to dream of finding a new way to treat cancer through the use of specially targeted immune cells, rather than more invasive treatments like radiotherapy, chemotherapy and operations.

On the stock market BioNTech is now worth more than Lufthansa and in 2020 Sahin and Türeci entered the list of the 100 richest Germans for the first time, with an estimated wealth of 2.4 billion euros. But people who know them say that money is not the reason why they do what they do. 'For Sahin, earning money has never been at the forefront of his thinking. His dream is to build something sustainable and lasting, by developing fundamentally new and improved therapies,' explained investor Thomas Strüngmann in a conversation with German journalists.

In the United States, it was Moncef Slaoui who was the Zoonotic-buster. He was born in Morocco, studied at the Free University of Brussels and worked in Belgium as head of the research department at GlaxoSmithKline before moving to the US at his own Slaoui Center for Vaccines Research in Maryland.

The man currently has fourteen marketed vaccines to his name, an impressive track record that few, if any, can match. It was perhaps no surprise that it was to Slaoui that the White House turned when it needed someone to head up 'Operation Warp Speed' (do you remember *Star Trek*?), whose mission was to develop and mass produce an effective COVID-19 vaccine within a year. He quickly realised that this mission not only involved a major scientific challenge, but also a logistical one. Developing the vaccine was just step one; getting it into people's arms was step two. The fact that he could rely on the unlimited support of logistical experts from the US military was a key factor in his final success, as was his realisation that there was no point in wasting energy by trying to go against the 'anti-science' attitude of the country's president. Instead, he set his focus on deciding quickly and decisively which of the trial vaccines had the most chance of success, so that these could be further tested without any loss of quality. The rest, as they say, is history.

Have you noticed how the profile of Zoonotic-busters like Slaoui and Sahin show many similarities with that of a Zoonotic leader? Or to put it in slightly different terms: whether you want to develop a Zoonotic business strategy of your own or a defence scenario to keep a Zoonotic at bay, in both cases you will need to possess the same leadership qualities as those I described in part 2.

How a Predatory Zoonotic can accelerate its own downfall

The highly aggressive approach of certain Zoonotics of the Uber-Robinhood type can actually help to bring about their own downfall. Similarly, the recent revelations about the way in which companies like Google and Facebook have used their knowledge of your surf-and-click history to successfully develop models that are not only able to predict your future behaviour, but also aim to 'kidnap'

EXPERT OPINION
Hans Peter Brøndmo
Computer scientist and tech entrepreneur

10x thinking

The Norwegian Hans Peter Brøndmo is another of the many fascinating people I met during my visit to Googleplex in California. He is in charge of the Everyday Robot Project, a robotics-meets-machine-learning moonshot for X, previously known as Google[x]. Brøndmo was a senior executive at Nokia/HERE, where he led the new product innovation business unit with teams in Silicon Valley, Germany, Finland and China. He also worked for Apple in Tokyo and even at CERN (Centre for European Nuclear Research) in Geneva. As if that were not enough, he is the author of the *New York Times* bestseller *The Engaged Customer*. Nowadays, Hans Peter is paid to play with robots. His motto:

> '10X thinking is often easier
> than 10% incremental thinking.
> You have to start all over
> with fresh thinking.'

'10X thinking' is about eliminating problems for billions of people via breakthrough technology that leads to radical solutions.

An innovative company culture challenges people, stimulates them to develop crazy ideas – because there is no such thing as a stupid question – and embraces mistakes. Innovation demands cognitive diversity. If all the various team leaders resemble each other, innovation becomes much harder. It was from him that I learnt the word 'tough-tech', meaning problems that you cannot solve with an app. He challenges us all to do a pre-mortem. Yes, a pre-mortem, not a post-mortem, because afterwards is always too late. You need to work out in advance where your project can go wrong.

> For him, Purpose and Profit are
> inseparable key concepts.
> Apart, neither of them is sustainable.

your attention more or less permanently, have caused a public outcry. All the more so since Tristan Harris, an ex-Google manager, announced at a conference in California that the metaphor used by the company to describe this system was 'voodoo doll'.

> 'I've accumulated all the ... clicks and likes you've ever made,
> and it makes this voodoo doll act more and more like you', said
> Harris. 'All I have to do is simulate what conversation the voodoo
> doll is having, and I know the conversation you will have.'

Harris went on to say that use of these 'voodoo dolls' was intended to capture the time and attention of Google users for as long as possible.

How long are we, the users, going to tolerate this creepy behaviour on the part of the arrogant, monopolistic tech giants? This form of 'Surveillance Capitalism' is a bad evolution. Consequently, I wish to emphasise the message of this book once again: namely, that companies must develop viral business strategies that are ethically responsible, with respect for the customers and for society. The time has come for us all to be aware that our data is as much ours as a part of our body, and not something to be sold on to third parties for profit without our knowledge and permission.

This is one of the greatest challenges and responsibilities facing the leaders of the big tech companies: to develop the necessary deontological codes at their own initiative, before the boomerang, albeit with far too much delay, hits them fair and square in the face as a result of government intervention.

In this respect, I fully share the wise words of Françoise Chombar. She definitely knows what she is talking about: under her leadership Melexis grew to become a company that currently has a stock market value of 3.854 billion dollars.

EXPERT OPINION

Françoise Chombar

Retiring CEO Melexis

'You can never trust technology completely. It is made by people and people are fallible. And just as well: otherwise, the world would be a very boring place. You always need to keep on using your brains. For me, people continue to be central. Technology is just a resource and must be used for the purposes of good.'

Government policy and Zoonotics?

In recent times we all witnessed at first hand the impact that a strong (or weak) government policy could have on the fight against corona. Might not a similarly strong government policy help to curb the excesses of the above-mentioned Predatory Zoonotics and what Shoshana Zuboff calls 'Surveillance Capitalism'? With this name, she is referring specifically to the big tech companies like Facebook, Amazon, Google and Apple, which have grown into powerful monopolists through the exploitation of our personal data. This, in combination with the Predator business model I described earlier, has resulted in the emergence in the United States of a growing number of activist groups that are starting to launch a counteroffensive. Their concerns have been taken up by the US Department of Justice, with the result that more and more legal cases are appearing before American courts to cut the digital giants down to size.

According to Roger McNamee, one of the most influential activists in this field, the government has a key role to play in this fight-back. After 40 years of deregulation, the time has come, says McNamee , to set clear limits to curb the abuses of these monopolistic companies. Not simply because their activities are not in the interests of consumers, but also because they widen the inequality gulf through the massive concentration of wealth in the hands of an ever-smaller group of people.

Because the algorithms of these companies give priority to opinions in preference to facts, they are an ideal breeding ground for fake news. The paradox is, however, that their very accessibility and ease of use means that the users willingly expose themselves without too much thought to the doubtful practices of the Predatory Zoonotics. Just try to avoid Google or YouTube. It is almost impossible. What's more, the corona pandemic has further enhanced the power of these giants, because it allowed them to rake in even more data and money. According to McNamee, only the government can stop them, by intervening in three key legislative areas:

1. **Anti-trust legislation.** In the past, the government has forced large petroleum and telecom companies to split up into smaller units. The same thing now needs to be done for the tech industry. McNamee refers, for example, to how the break-up of AT&T and IBM gave the chance to other companies to develop new services.

2. **Privacy legislation.** McNamee argues that our personal data should not be regarded as an asset that the tech companies can trade at will, but as something owned by the person in question that can only be traded under that person's conditions.

3. **Safety legislation.** Just as an architect who designs a new bridge or a pharmaceutical company that markets a new medicine are liable for any errors or negative effects resulting from their activities, so the tech companies should likewise be made liable for any errors or negative effects resulting from the services and applications they develop.

Similarly, the excesses of the sharing economy are also worthy of the government's attention. Think, for example, of Spotify and musicians' royalties; or the impact of Airbnb on rental prices, so that poorer residents are being driven out of some towns and cities; or the poor working conditions and inadequate social protection of the people employed by Uber or Deliveroo. The government needs to ensure that there is a level playing field for all concerned. That, after all, is its job.

INSIGHT

> **The Chinese government clips the wings of Alibaba sister AliPay**

If you want to see a powerful example of State Capitalism in action, look no further than the way in which the Chinese authorities intervened to compel the financial group of Alibaba founder Jack Ma to restructure its operational activities. Ma was forced to set up a separate holding company to guarantee that the group would have sufficient capital to prevent problems and ensure compliance with the relevant legislation. The banking group was also obliged to revise its systems for credit assessment, insurance and capital management, so that the personal data of customers was better protected. In concrete terms, this means that in future the state will be looking more closely over the shoulders of the tech giants, particularly Alibaba and Tencent, to put a check on their monopolisitc activities and prevent their further acquisition of power.

In addition, the government can also play an important role in 'identity portability', which would make it possible for you to transfer all your data from one service provider to another. During my time at Proximus, I saw at first hand how the possibility for a customer to keep the same mobile phone number when switching to a different mobile provider had a huge impact on breaking open the market for new players. So imagine what it could mean for you if it was possible to transfer all your Facebook data and all your friends quickly and easily to another service provider like, say, LinkedIn? In Europe, steps are already being taken to investigate to what extent your ownership rights to your own data can be better protected. A positive move in the direction of identity portability would be certain to significantly weaken the position of Facebook and other similar companies.

The legislative power could also make possible the obligatory opening of existing networks or the obligatory sub-division of mega-corporations, which would lower the threshold for new start-ups and give them a better chance of success. The excuse put forward by Mark Zuckerberg for buying WhatsApp – that it was otherwise impossible to integrate it into Facebook – was clearly a fallacy, because within a few months that integration was a reality.

In the absence of these kinds of legal initiatives, the giants of the tech industry, who themselves were once innovative, make sure that today's innovative start-ups are hardly ever given the chance to develop. And that, in turn, results in a serious distortion of the free market.

Financial analysts are of the opinion that it would actually be in the interests of Facebook, or rather its shareholders, to give up its legal battles and to reach an agreement about the splitting up of the company into separate units. When Standard Oil was similarly split some years ago, it simply served to make John D. Rockefeller even richer. So, hey Mark, what are you waiting for? The sub-division of the digital monopolist would no doubt be a good thing for everyone.

EXPERT OPINION

Peter De Keyzer
Founder and managing partner, Growth Inc.

Dealing with unknown uncertainties
'We feel comfortable when we are dealing with known certainties, because they are relatively easy to predict and to process in scenarios. What we have trouble with are "unknown uncertainties".

Dealing with the unexpected is totally different from compiling quarterly reports and spreadsheets. The unexpected demands flexibility, improvisation, resilience and leadership. The pandemic has actually brought the true nature of people, companies and government authorities to the surface. The countries that are in essence methodical and well structured have come through the crisis relatively unscathed. In other words, it is not really a surprise that Belgium has failed to score well in this respect. We pay high rates of tax and get little in return. Corona has made this discrepancy even clearer. We do not have a sufficiently long-term perspective. We cannot move up through the gears quickly enough.

Everyone is authorised,
but no one is responsible

This has strengthened the realisation that we need to be better prepared to respond to "unknown uncertainties". Before the crisis, there were hundreds of reports available in which countless future trends were predicted, but the less predictable risk of a pandemic was hardly mentioned at all. We are much too concerned about "the flavour of the day". If you look at the themes that were on the agenda in recent years at Davos, they were usually the themes that had been current the year before! That, however, is only human. We seldom occupy ourselves with the distant future or radical scenarios. They all seem so very far away.

As a result, no one saw the pandemic coming. Okay, perhaps that is understandable. But if companies failed to respond quickly once the crisis hit, that was the result of the nature and attitudes of their leaders. To make matters worse, many companies and people are useless when left to their own devices and instantly turn to the government for solutions to their problems.

Fortunately, people like Alexander De Croo and Frank Vandenbroucke dare to show true leadership and are willing to take often unpopular decisions. Similarly in the business world, there were some brave souls who succeeded in reinventing themselves and setting an example for others. Consider, for instance, Ronny Bayens, the CEO of Connections. As soon as he saw that a lockdown was inevitable, he quickly purchased 130 laptops, so that his personnel could work from home. Within just a few days, these computers were all formatted correctly. He did not freeze when faced with uncertainty. Instead, he rolled up his sleeves and by the time summer arrived had built brand-new luxury camping in Durbuy. He even helped to erect and decorate the tents! Likewise, in the event world Golazo reacted at speed and transformed itself into a creator of virtual sports competitions and apps. Their expertise was also useful when it came to setting up the COVID-19 triage centre in Antwerp. Many restaurants also demonstrated commendable speed by quickly converting into take-away outlets.

Regrettably, some well-intentioned initiatives were blocked by the short-sightedness of government policy. Take, for example, the idea of the test bus. This was the brainchild of a number of entrepreneurs from East Flanders and was intended to give companies, schools and local authorities the chance to offer mobile corona testing on site. It was a great private initiative, but one that was blocked because it did not comply 100 percent with the letter of government regulations

The true extent of the economic consequences of the corona pandemic will only become fully apparent once it is over. It is to be hoped that the government will then have the courage to separate the wheat from the chaff and will not continue to support companies that clearly have no viable future in the new economic context.

Conclusions? The most important thing is to train your management to deal with "unpredictable uncertainties". That is also how armies train their elite troops. Coping with stress and uncertainty is second nature to them. Previously announced training programmes are regularly turned upside down by their commanders. Why? Because the new recruits need to be confronted with the unexpected. Learning how to react to it is crucial for the development of the necessary agility and resilience. I think that corona has taught us that this also needs to be the case for our business leaders.'

VOLVO EPIC SPLIT

In a video clip Jean-Claude Van Damme demonstrates his legendary split while standing on the wing mirrors of two Volvo lorries reversing slowly away from each other. With this stunt Volvo wanted to highlight the precision and safety of its new dynamic steering system. The resulting images were spectacular and certainly appealed to the imagination. What's more, the dramatic effect was heightened by the use of the right music. The stunt – at first, many people thought that it had been faked – was performed live by Van Damme in a single take. After just one day, the clip had been viewed more than 6 million times and given over 52,000 likes.

It cost between 3 and 4 million dollars to make, but yielded Volvo an additional turnover estimated at 170 million dollars. A survey among buyers revealed that half had followed the test live and that a third had contacted a Volvo dealer shortly afterwards. The clip was also the talk of the town amongst these dealers, who operate in over 140 countries. It was often the first thing that potential customers mentioned when they visited a Volvo showroom.

1. What is the creative idea and who benefits from it?

How can you get people all around the world talking about lorries? By moving the focus away from the product itself and focusing on the relevance of the message for the core target group – the lorry drivers – while at the same time making the story sufficiently attractive for a wider public because of its dramatic effect. Forsman & Bodenfors advertising agency initially thought that Volvo needed the services of a B-2-B agency, until it became clear that the company had a totally different approach in mind. The buyers of lorries are influenced by a number of different people, including (to a significant degree) their fellow truckers. But those are the people that you are not going to reach with a classic media campaign. In view of the relatively limited budget for an international campaign, a viral business strategy was the only viable approach.

2. What stimulates people to take part and share the idea?

The message was adjusted and attuned to the different channels that were used. The aim was amaze the surfer, so that he/she would react with a comment and/or by sharing.

3. How can you use time pressure to speed up the process?

Neuro-research has shown that it is above all women whose curiosity is stimulated by a split, whereas the men tend to concentrate on the pain they think Jean-Claude Van Damme must have experienced. As a result, the core message – the precision and safety of the steering system – was well remembered.

4. How can you get the support of big names?

The tough macho figure of Jean-Claude Van Damme, famous for his splits in his 'hard-man' films, was a perfect match for the core target group.

5. How can you use short and memorable videos and photos?

At that time, the use of YouTube for viral marketing was still relatively new. The video started as a paid advertisement, but very soon began to live a virtual life of its own.

6. How does the campaign motivate engagement?

The video emphasises the importance of the precision steering system for road safety.

7. How can you keep the threshold for participation as low as possible?

The video clip is built up as a spectacular and exciting film, a real thriller, which holds people's attention from beginning to end.

cHeCKLisT

MAKE WORK OF DEVELOPING AN INFLUENCER MARKETING STRATEGY, AND DO IT NOW.

- WHEN THE ZOONOTIC STRIKES, IT IS ALREADY TOO LATE.
- IT TAKES TIME TO BUILD UP A MUTUAL RELATIONSHIP OF TRUST WITH INFLUENCERS.
- INFLUENCERS CAN ACT AS EARLY-WARNERS FOR THE APPROACH OF A ZOONOTIC.
- THEY CAN ALSO SERVE AS A PROTECTIVE SHIELD.

WHEN THE ZOONOTIC STRIKES, YOU WILL FIND YOURSELF IN A SANDSTORM.

- WHO IS AUTHORISED TO WIELD THE HAMMER?
- WHO WILL LEAD THE DANCE?

PREPARE YOUR DEFENCE SCENARIO AGAINST A ZOONOTIC ATTACK.

- DEVELOP A SYSTEM OF FAST TRACING AND REPORTING.
- USE REAL-TIME WARGAME EXERCISES TO PRACTISE.

IF THERE IS ANYTHING I CAN DO

In contrast to my previous two books, this one was written during a highly challenging period, not only for myself, my company and my team, but also for billions of people and millions of other businesses all around our vulnerable blue planet. It is part of my nature as an optimistic entrepreneur and strategic thinker that even in those confusing and uncertain times I was keen to search for the lessons that could be learned, often hidden beneath the disruptive waves of what we now generally know as the corona crisis.

This is not a scientific book, but I hope that I have succeeded in my desire to illustrate my basic point clearly; namely, that a pandemic offers important insights that can inspire us to develop a successful viral business strategy.

If you are able to bring together two existing Unfair Advantages and combine them to create something completely new, this will make it possible, with the help of a Superspreader, for your viral strategy to conquer the world at an exponential speed, just like a Zoonotic.

This requires a Zoonotic leader with vision and grit. 'The misfit. The rebel. The troublemaker. The round peg in the square hole. The one who sees things differently,' as the famous Apple commercial puts it. He or she often generates a considerable amount of friction with regard to the existing processes and usages in the company, especially because the Zoonotic leader is frequently younger and therefore has less leadership experience.

The many examples in this book show that no company can afford to rest on its laurels and think: 'This can never happen to us'. Because a viral Zoonotic business strategy usually starts life as an almost invisible, slumbering singularity, it does not immediately appear on people's radars or, if it does, it seems too insignificant to be worthy of much attention. But by then it is often already too late, because once the Zoonotic starts its exponential march of conquest, it is almost impossible to stop.

Almost, but not quite. Hence this passionate plea: you must either become a Zoonotic leader yourself or must have the courage to give a Zoonotic leader in your company the necessary space to develop. Because even if you cannot become a Zoonotic, but only wish to survive a Zoonotic attack (as far as this is possible), you will still need a Zoonotic-buster who has precisely the same qualities as a Zoonotic leader.

Together with my team, I am ready, willing and available to help you. 'If there is anything that you want, if there is anything I can do, just call on me and I'll send it along, with love from me to you...'

Carole

BIBLIOGRAPHY

Bruelemans, Bart, Brugghemans, Bert & Van Mechelen, Ilse, *Help! Een crisis*, die Keure, 2015

Courtney, Emily, *27 companies that have switched to long-term remote work*, Flexjobs blogpost

De Schepper, Jan, Van Den Bosch, Paul, *Connexion*, Lannoo Campus, 2021

Downes, Larry, Nunes, Paul, *Big Bang Disruption*, Accenture Singularity University, SUBlog

Duckworth, Angela, *Grit: The power of passion and perseverence*, TED talk

Ingels, Jurgen, *'Creativiteit is nu al belangrijker dan technologie'*, podcast De Tijd Vooruit, 22 October 2020

Ipsos Marketing, *Point of view, Discovering what people want before they do*, 2012

Lamarque, Carole, *Influencers*, LannooCampus, 2017

Lamarque, Carole, *Unfair Advantage*, LannooCampus, 2019

Piot, Peter, *'Dit is the Big One'*, podcast De Tijd Vooruit, 22 October 2020

Pueyo, Tomas, *Coronavirus: The hammer and the dance*, tomaspuyeo.medium. com

Raworth, Kate, *Donut Economie*, Nieuw Amsterdam, 2019

Schwab, Klaus, *Davos Manifesto 2020: The Universal Purpose of a Company in the Fourth Industrial Revolution*

The Mozilla Foundation, https://foundation.mozilla.org

Van Dyck, Fons, *'Vivaldi kan inspiratie opdoen bij The Beatles'*, De Tijd, 14 October 2020

Wagemans, Wibe, Schram, Eva, *The secret of Silicon Valley*, 2020, e-book

Zuboff Shoshana, *The Age of Surveillance Capitalism*, Profile Books Ltd, 2019